malcolm & Lauren gave this
to me   2005
return from q.

The Pillows to Patch Quilt Collection
...the Hawaiian Way

32 Original Designs by
Elizabeth Root

Illustrations by
Tammy Yee

ERDHI

2

Quilt designs
Copyright ©2002 Elizabeth Root
Illustrations and drawings
Copyright ©2002
Elizabeth Root Designs Hawaii, Inc.

Designs previously published as
Pillows to Patch Quilt I ©1998
Pillows to Patch Quilt II ©1998
Pillows to Kapohopoho ©1994
Pillows to Patchwork ©1994

Color illustrations by Tammy Yee
Photography by Paul Kodama
Pre-press by Kym Miller/Kymaging

Library of Congress Catalog
Card Number 2002090298

Softcover
ISBN 1-885804-05-9

Printed in China
10 9 8 7 6 5 4

The pillows shown in this book were all made by a group of needle women who have been doing fine hand appliqué and quilting for me since 1990.

ERDHI
Elizabeth Root Designs Hawaii, Inc.
Post Office Box 1167
Kailua, HI 96734
email: pillows@quiltshawaii.com
www.quiltshawaii.com

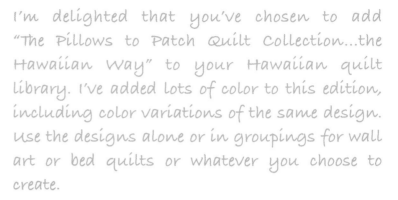

Aloha from Elizabeth

I'm delighted that you've chosen to add "The Pillows to Patch Quilt Collection...the Hawaiian Way" to your Hawaiian quilt library. I've added lots of color to this edition, including color variations of the same design. Use the designs alone or in groupings for wall art or bed quilts or whatever you choose to create.

Hawaiian quilt designs are not just for Hawaii, nor are they only made using solid colored fabrics anymore. Use whatever you like in prints, textures and types of fabric to create a Hawaiian quilt masterpiece that will blend or coordinate with any style or decor, anywhere.

Enjoy!

Table of Contents

4

Table of Contents

Table of Contents

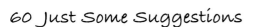

FABRIC NEEDED - size after preshrinking

Each of the designs in this book is 18" square. This means you should use the following as guidelines if making them one color appliqué designs in the same size. These are generous allowances.

Appliqué fabric color:	1 - 15" to 16" square
Background fabric color:	1 - 20" to 21" square
Backing fabric color:	1 - 21" square; can match any of the fabric colors used for the front. If using as a wall hanging, a solid color will best show the quilting.
Muslin backing:	1 - 21" square; if making a pillow, use a piece of muslin or cotton and save the background fabric to finish the back of the pillow.
Batting:	1 - 22" square; depending upon the thickness of your batting, when quilted, it may become smaller; so be sure that you have adequate allowance.

 REMEMBER, you can always cut off the excess fabric, but using too little fabric can not be reversed. Always preshrink your fabric, if necessary.

WORKING WITH MULTICOLOR DESIGNS

Each pattern that lends itself to multicolor appliqué has a second multi-color cutting pattern. You may want to cut those separately from smaller squares of fabric and then place them separately. Keep in mind that if you fold the smaller piece of fabric in eighths and then cut it, it will be easier to place the pieces because you will have the fold line to guide you.

You should pin each color in place, keeping in mind the layering – e.g., usually flowers will be appliquéd over stems that are part of the leaf color; a planter over a stem; a flower over a center color. But if the flower has a "stem" of the same color, then it will usually go under the leaf. Think of how you would view these things in nature and let that be your guide.

FABRICS

There is a wealth of wonderful fabrics on the market today. Take advantage of different prints, textures and types of fabrics. Hawaiian quilting is not just for solid colored fabrics anymore. You can use fabrics that best suit your decor, combining solids with prints that coordinate nicely with your bedroom and living areas. Remember, just because these are Hawaiian quilt designs, it doesn't mean that they won't work beautifully with any decor and color scheme, anywhere.

The Designs

and Patterns

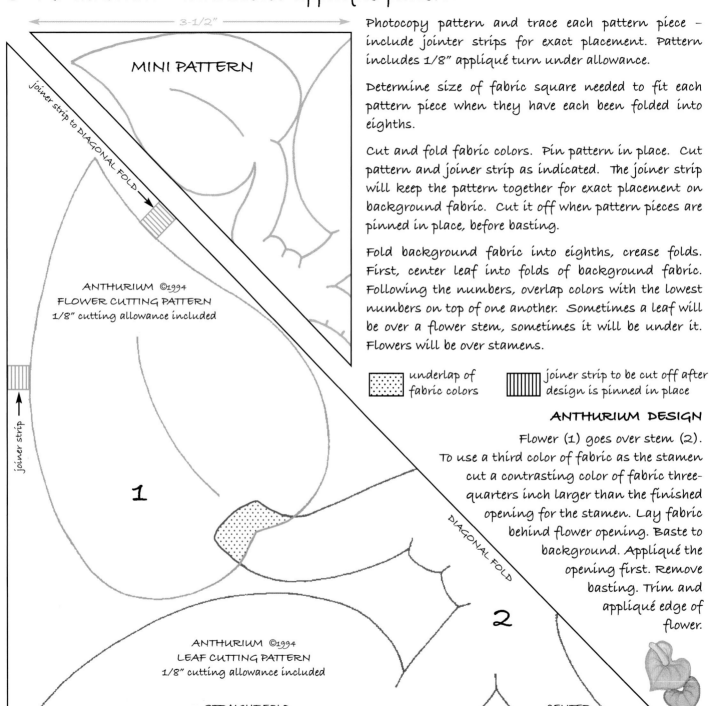

MINI PATTERN

Joiner strip to DIAGONAL FOLD →

joiner strip

ANTHURIUM ©1994
FLOWER CUTTING PATTERN
1/8" cutting allowance included

1

3-1/2"

ANTHURIUM ©1994
LEAF CUTTING PATTERN
1/8" cutting allowance included

STRAIGHT FOLD

DIAGONAL FOLD

2

CENTER

7"

Photocopy pattern and trace each pattern piece – include jointer strips for exact placement. Pattern includes 1/8" appliqué turn under allowance.

Determine size of fabric square needed to fit each pattern piece when they have each been folded into eighths.

Cut and fold fabric colors. Pin pattern in place. Cut pattern and joiner strip as indicated. The joiner strip will keep the pattern together for exact placement on background fabric. Cut it off when pattern pieces are pinned in place, before basting.

Fold background fabric into eighths, crease folds. First, center leaf into folds of background fabric. Following the numbers, overlap colors with the lowest numbers on top of one another. Sometimes a leaf will be over a flower stem, sometimes it will be under it. Flowers will be over stamens.

:::: underlap of fabric colors

||||| joiner strip to be cut off after design is pinned in place

ANTHURIUM DESIGN

Flower (1) goes over stem (2). To use a third color of fabric as the stamen cut a contrasting color of fabric three-quarters inch larger than the finished opening for the stamen. Lay fabric behind flower opening. Baste to background. Appliqué the opening first. Remove basting. Trim and appliqué edge of flower.

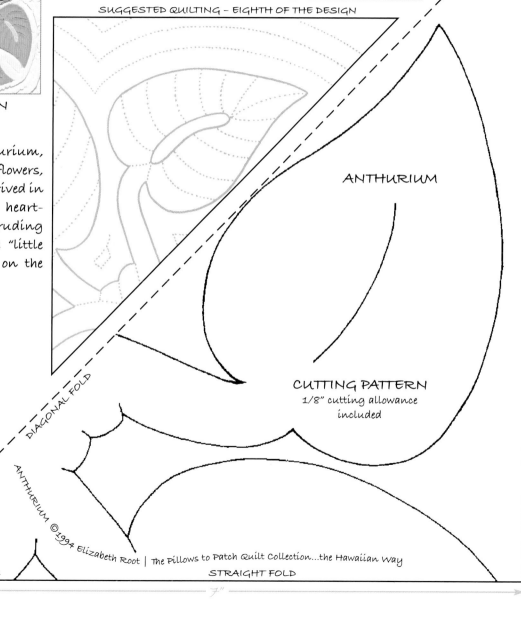

SUGGESTED QUILTING – EIGHTH OF THE DESIGN

ADVANCED PATTERN

ANTHURIUM

The first anthurium, with shell-pink flowers, is said to have arrived in Hawaii in 1889. These heart-shaped flowers with protruding stamen (locally called the "little boy flower") last months on the plant, many weeks cut.

Companion Piece:
Bird of Paradise,
Page 11

ANTHURIUM

CUTTING PATTERN
1/8" cutting allowance
included

DIAGONAL FOLD

ANTHURIUM

ANTHURIUM ©1994 Elizabeth Root | The Pillows to Patch Quilt Collection...the Hawaiian Way

CENTER

STRAIGHT FOLD

7"

10 Autograph Leaf

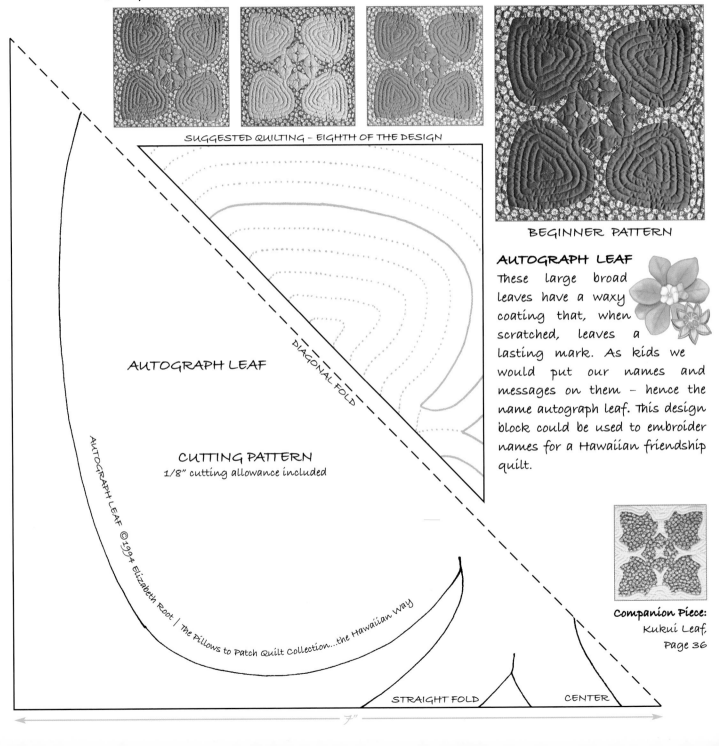

SUGGESTED QUILTING – EIGHTH OF THE DESIGN

BEGINNER PATTERN

DIAGONAL FOLD

AUTOGRAPH LEAF

CUTTING PATTERN
1/8" cutting allowance included

AUTOGRAPH LEAF ©1994 Elizabeth Root | The Pillows to Patch Quilt Collection...the Hawaiian Way

STRAIGHT FOLD   CENTER

7"

AUTOGRAPH LEAF

These large broad leaves have a waxy coating that, when scratched, leaves a lasting mark. As kids we would put our names and messages on them – hence the name autograph leaf. This design block could be used to embroider names for a Hawaiian friendship quilt.

Companion Piece:
Kukui Leaf,
Page 36

ADVANCED PATTERN

BIRD OF PARADISE

The bird of paradise is one of the showiest of Hawaii's tropical flowers with its brightly colored orange petals amidst dark, forest green leaves. It is used in floral arrangements as it will last as long as two weeks cut.

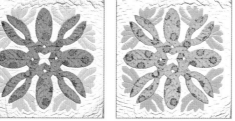

SUGGESTED QUILTING – EIGHTH OF THE DESIGN

STAMEN

BIRD OF PARADISE

BIRD OF PARADISE

DIAGONAL FOLD

CUTTING PATTERN
1/8" cutting allowance included

Companion Piece:
Anthurium,
Page 8

BIRD OF PARADISE ©1994 Elizabeth Root | The Pillows to Patch Quilt Collection...the Hawaiian Way

CENTER   STRAIGHT FOLD

7"

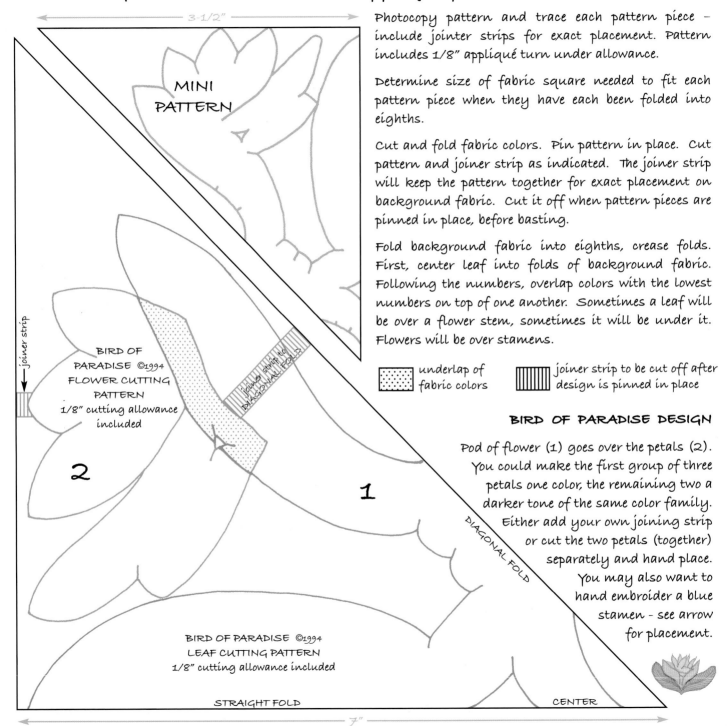

Photocopy pattern and trace each pattern piece – include jointer strips for exact placement. Pattern includes 1/8" appliqué turn under allowance.

Determine size of fabric square needed to fit each pattern piece when they have each been folded into eighths.

Cut and fold fabric colors. Pin pattern in place. Cut pattern and joiner strip as indicated. The joiner strip will keep the pattern together for exact placement on background fabric. Cut it off when pattern pieces are pinned in place, before basting.

Fold background fabric into eighths, crease folds. First, center leaf into folds of background fabric. Following the numbers, overlap colors with the lowest numbers on top of one another. Sometimes a leaf will be over a flower stem, sometimes it will be under it. Flowers will be over stamens.

underlap of fabric colors

joiner strip to be cut off after design is pinned in place

BIRD OF PARADISE DESIGN

Pod of flower (1) goes over the petals (2). You could make the first group of three petals one color, the remaining two a darker tone of the same color family. Either add your own joining strip or cut the two petals (together) separately and hand place. You may also want to hand embroider a blue stamen - see arrow for placement.

MINI PATTERN

3-1/2"

joiner strip

BIRD OF PARADISE ©1994 FLOWER CUTTING PATTERN 1/8" cutting allowance included

2

joiner strip to DIAGONAL FOLD

1

DIAGONAL FOLD

BIRD OF PARADISE ©1994 LEAF CUTTING PATTERN 1/8" cutting allowance included

STRAIGHT FOLD

CENTER

7"

BEGINNER PATTERN

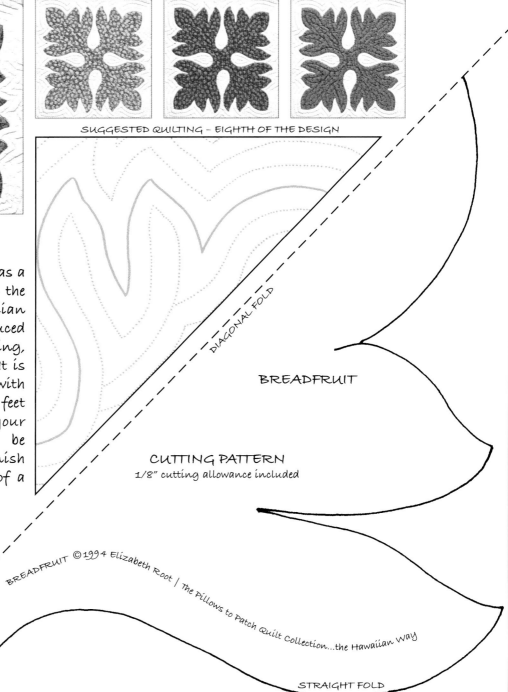

SUGGESTED QUILTING – EIGHTH OF THE DESIGN

BREADFRUIT

The breadfruit was a major staple in the early Hawaiian diet. It also produced wood for canoes, sap for gluing, and a chewing-like gum. It is a majestic tree with leaves with broad leathery leaves 1-3 feet long. It is said that your Hawaiian quilting will be bountiful when you finish your design that is part of a breadfruit tree.

DIAGONAL FOLD

BREADFRUIT

CUTTING PATTERN
1/8" cutting allowance included

BREADFRUIT ©1994 Elizabeth Root | The Pillows to Patch Quilt Collection...the Hawaiian Way

Companion Piece:
Fern Laua'e,
Page 22

CENTER

STRAIGHT FOLD

7"

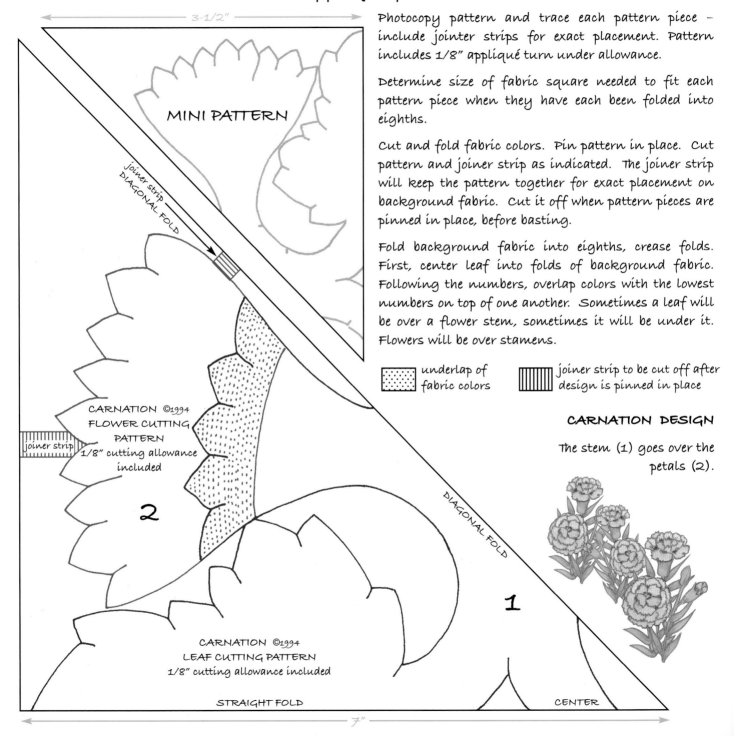

3-1/2"

MINI PATTERN

Joiner strip
DIAGONAL FOLD

CARNATION ©1994
FLOWER CUTTING
PATTERN
1/8" cutting allowance
included

joiner strip

2

DIAGONAL FOLD

1

CARNATION ©1994
LEAF CUTTING PATTERN
1/8" cutting allowance included

STRAIGHT FOLD

CENTER

7"

Photocopy pattern and trace each pattern piece – include jointer strips for exact placement. Pattern includes 1/8" appliqué turn under allowance.

Determine size of fabric square needed to fit each pattern piece when they have each been folded into eighths.

Cut and fold fabric colors. Pin pattern in place. Cut pattern and joiner strip as indicated. The joiner strip will keep the pattern together for exact placement on background fabric. Cut it off when pattern pieces are pinned in place, before basting.

Fold background fabric into eighths, crease folds. First, center leaf into folds of background fabric. Following the numbers, overlap colors with the lowest numbers on top of one another. Sometimes a leaf will be over a flower stem, sometimes it will be under it. Flowers will be over stamens.

underlap of fabric colors

joiner strip to be cut off after design is pinned in place

CARNATION DESIGN

The stem (1) goes over the petals (2).

ADVANCED PATTERN

CARNATION

The carnation's Hawaiian name Poni Mo'i means "coronation of the king." Its flowers are used in leis. How important we felt getting a massive triple carnation lei at graduation. A special coloring of red petals striped with white is called "Hawaiian Flag" – a favorite in Hawaii.

Companion Piece:
Lehua,
Page 37

SUGGESTED QUILTING – EIGHTH OF THE DESIGN

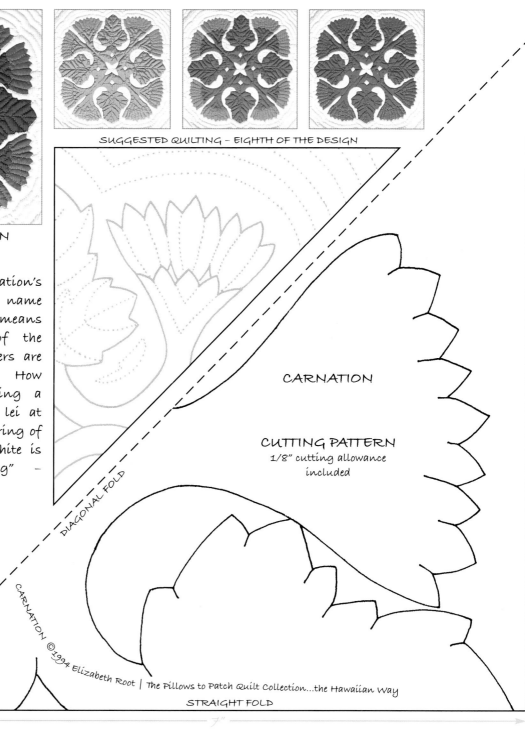

CARNATION

CUTTING PATTERN
1/8" cutting allowance
included

DIAGONAL FOLD

CARNATION ©1994 Elizabeth Root | The Pillows to Patch Quilt Collection...the Hawaiian Way

CENTER

STRAIGHT FOLD

7"

16 Chrysanthemum – multicolor appliqué pattern

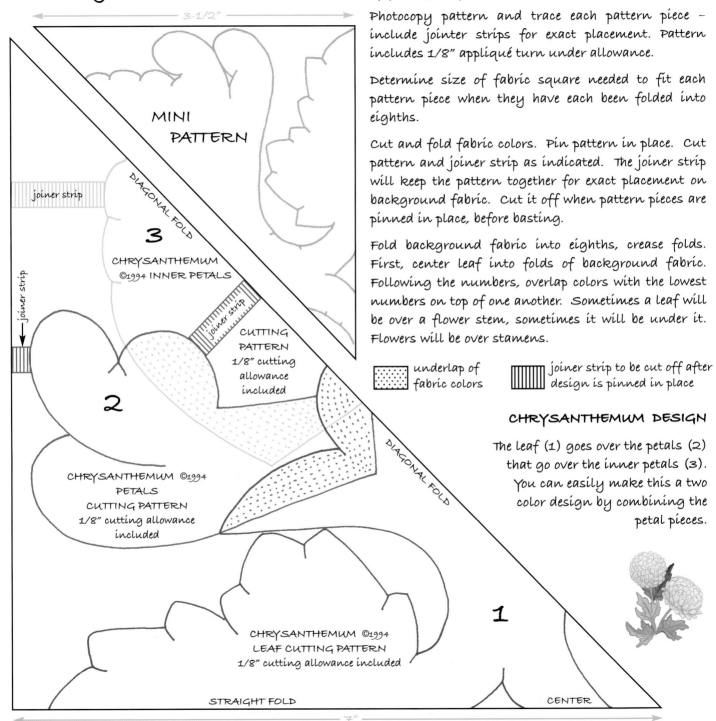

3-1/2"

MINI PATTERN

DIAGONAL FOLD

joiner strip

joiner strip

joiner strip

3

CHRYSANTHEMUM
©1994 INNER PETALS

CUTTING
PATTERN
1/8" cutting
allowance
included

2

CHRYSANTHEMUM ©1994
PETALS
CUTTING PATTERN
1/8" cutting allowance
included

DIAGONAL FOLD

1

CHRYSANTHEMUM ©1994
LEAF CUTTING PATTERN
1/8" cutting allowance included

STRAIGHT FOLD

CENTER

7"

Photocopy pattern and trace each pattern piece – include jointer strips for exact placement. Pattern includes 1/8" appliqué turn under allowance.

Determine size of fabric square needed to fit each pattern piece when they have each been folded into eighths.

Cut and fold fabric colors. Pin pattern in place. Cut pattern and joiner strip as indicated. The joiner strip will keep the pattern together for exact placement on background fabric. Cut it off when pattern pieces are pinned in place, before basting.

Fold background fabric into eighths, crease folds. First, center leaf into folds of background fabric. Following the numbers, overlap colors with the lowest numbers on top of one another. Sometimes a leaf will be over a flower stem, sometimes it will be under it. Flowers will be over stamens.

underlap of fabric colors

joiner strip to be cut off after design is pinned in place

CHRYSANTHEMUM DESIGN

The leaf (1) goes over the petals (2) that go over the inner petals (3). You can easily make this a two color design by combining the petal pieces.

ADVANCED PATTERN

SUGGESTED QUILTING – EIGHTH OF THE DESIGN

CHRYSANTHEMUM

Pua Pake, loosely translated means Chinese flower and was probably brought to Hawaii from China. The magnificent showy blooms are used in floral arrangements and are a popular Hawaiian quilt design.

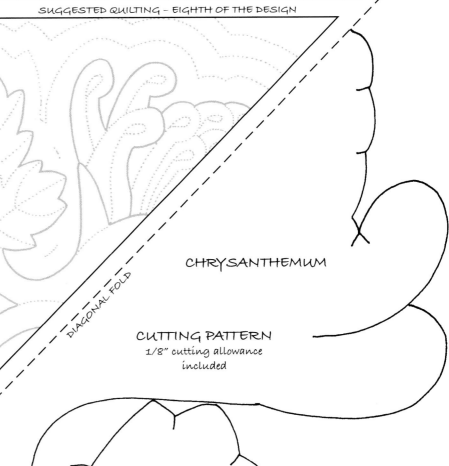

DIAGONAL FOLD

CHRYSANTHEMUM

CUTTING PATTERN
1/8" cutting allowance
included

CHRYSANTHEMUM ©1994 Elizabeth Root | The Pillows to Patch Quilt Collection...the Hawaiian Way

CENTER

STRAIGHT FOLD

7"

Companion Piece:
Hibiscus,
Page 32

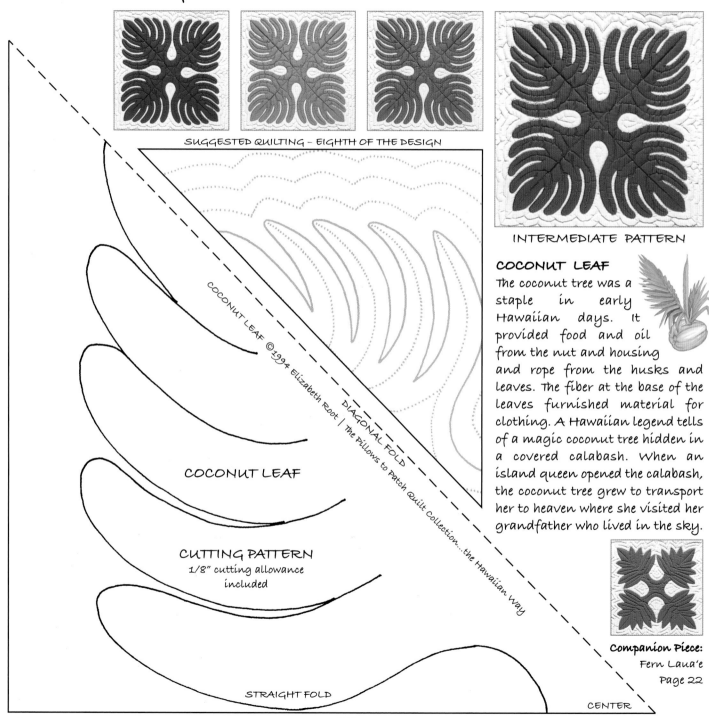

SUGGESTED QUILTING – EIGHTH OF THE DESIGN

INTERMEDIATE PATTERN

COCONUT LEAF ©1994 Elizabeth Root | The Pillows to Patch Quilt Collection...the Hawaiian Way

COCONUT LEAF

DIAGONAL FOLD

COCONUT LEAF

CUTTING PATTERN
1/8" cutting allowance
included

STRAIGHT FOLD

CENTER

7"

COCONUT LEAF

The coconut tree was a staple in early Hawaiian days. It provided food and oil from the nut and housing and rope from the husks and leaves. The fiber at the base of the leaves furnished material for clothing. A Hawaiian legend tells of a magic coconut tree hidden in a covered calabash. When an island queen opened the calabash, the coconut tree grew to transport her to heaven where she visited her grandfather who lived in the sky.

Companion Piece:
Fern Laua'e
Page 22

BEGINNER PATTERN

SUGGESTED QUILTING – EIGHTH OF THE DESIGN

CROWN FLOWER

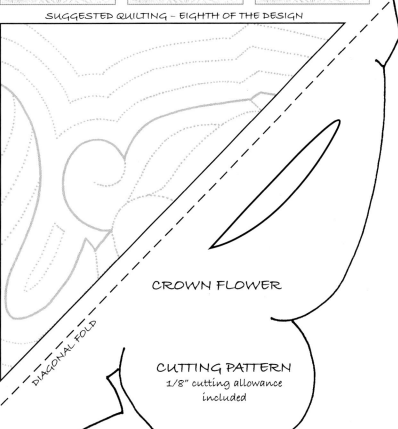

When I was a child, my father built me a wonderful play-house from some packing crates. The windows looked out on crown flower plants where I spent endless hours watching the big fuzzy caterpillars build their cocoons on the cream or lavender flower-laden branches to emerge as Hawaii's mock "Monarch" Butterfly.

DIAGONAL FOLD

CROWN FLOWER

CUTTING PATTERN
1/8" cutting allowance included

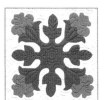

Companion Piece:
Lokelani Rose
Page 39

CENTER

CROWN FLOWER ©1994 Elizabeth Root | The Pillows to Patch Quilt Collection...the Hawaiian Way

STRAIGHT FOLD

7"

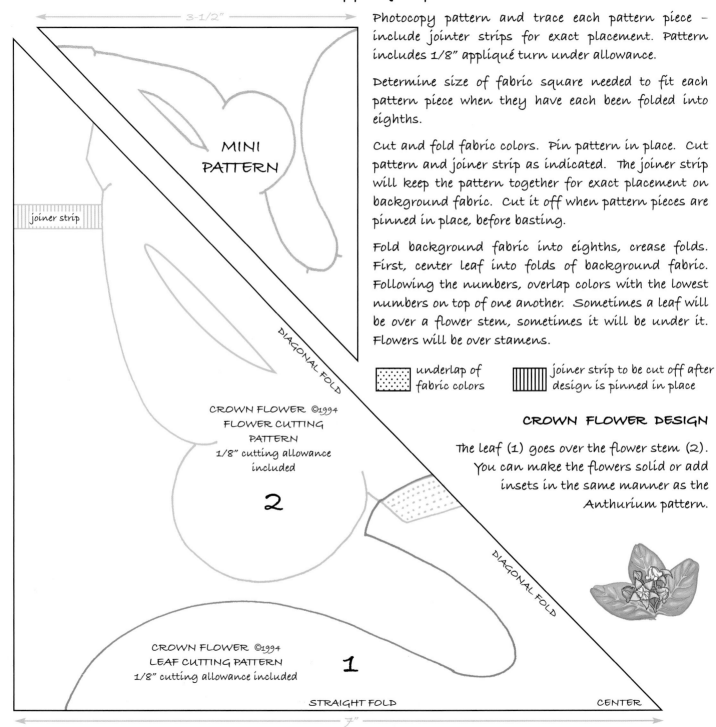

3-1/2"

MINI
PATTERN

joiner strip

DIAGONAL FOLD

CROWN FLOWER ©1994
FLOWER CUTTING
PATTERN
1/8" cutting allowance
included

2

CROWN FLOWER ©1994
LEAF CUTTING PATTERN
1/8" cutting allowance included

1

STRAIGHT FOLD

CENTER

7"

Photocopy pattern and trace each pattern piece – include joiner strips for exact placement. Pattern includes 1/8" appliqué turn under allowance.

Determine size of fabric square needed to fit each pattern piece when they have each been folded into eighths.

Cut and fold fabric colors. Pin pattern in place. Cut pattern and joiner strip as indicated. The joiner strip will keep the pattern together for exact placement on background fabric. Cut it off when pattern pieces are pinned in place, before basting.

Fold background fabric into eighths, crease folds. First, center leaf into folds of background fabric. Following the numbers, overlap colors with the lowest numbers on top of one another. Sometimes a leaf will be over a flower stem, sometimes it will be under it. Flowers will be over stamens.

underlap of fabric colors   joiner strip to be cut off after design is pinned in place

CROWN FLOWER DESIGN

The leaf (1) goes over the flower stem (2). You can make the flowers solid or add insets in the same manner as the Anthurium pattern.

DIAGONAL FOLD

BEGINNER PATTERN

SUGGESTED QUILTING – EIGHTH OF THE DESIGN

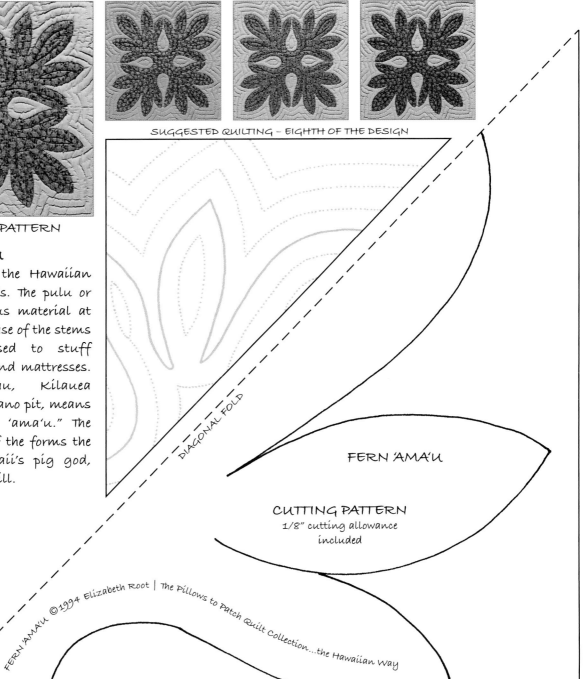

FERN 'AMA'U

Endemic to the Hawaiian Islands. The pulu or fibrous material at the base of the stems was used to stuff pillows and mattresses. Halemaumau, Kilauea crater's active volcano pit, means the "home of the 'ama'u." The 'ama'u was one of the forms the Kamapua'a, Hawaii's pig god, could assume at will.

Companion Piece:
Tí Leaf,
Page 56

DIAGONAL FOLD

FERN 'AMA'U

CUTTING PATTERN
1/8" cutting allowance
included

FERN 'AMA'U ©1994 Elizabeth Root | The Pillows to Patch Quilt Collection...the Hawaiian Way

CENTER

STRAIGHT FOLD

7"

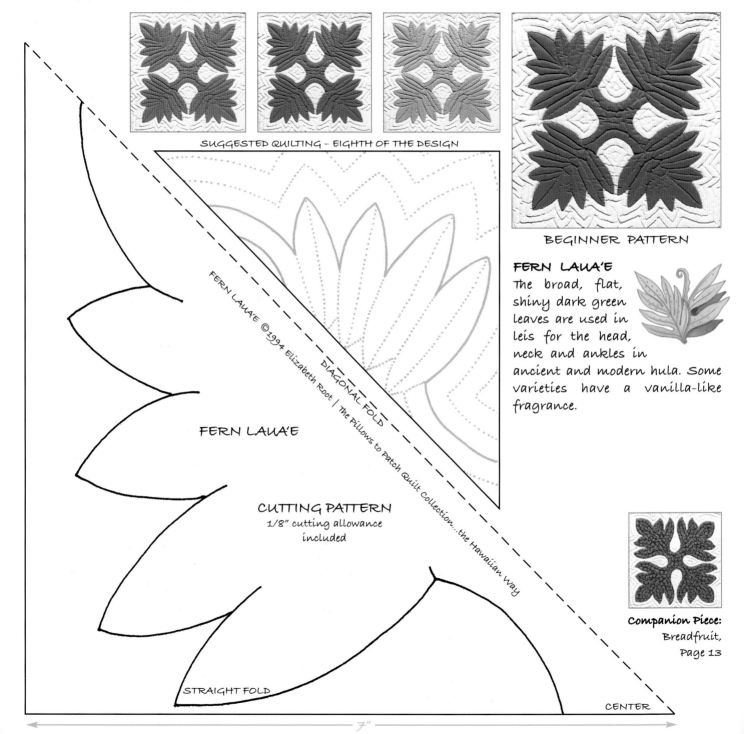

SUGGESTED QUILTING – EIGHTH OF THE DESIGN

BEGINNER PATTERN

FERN LAUA'E
The broad, flat, shiny dark green leaves are used in leis for the head, neck and ankles in ancient and modern hula. Some varieties have a vanilla-like fragrance.

FERN LAUA'E ©1994 Elizabeth Root | The Pillows to Patch Quilt Collection...the Hawaiian Way

DIAGONAL FOLD

FERN LAUA'E

CUTTING PATTERN
1/8" cutting allowance
included

STRAIGHT FOLD

CENTER

7"

Companion Piece:
Breadfruit,
Page 13

INTERMEDIATE PATTERN

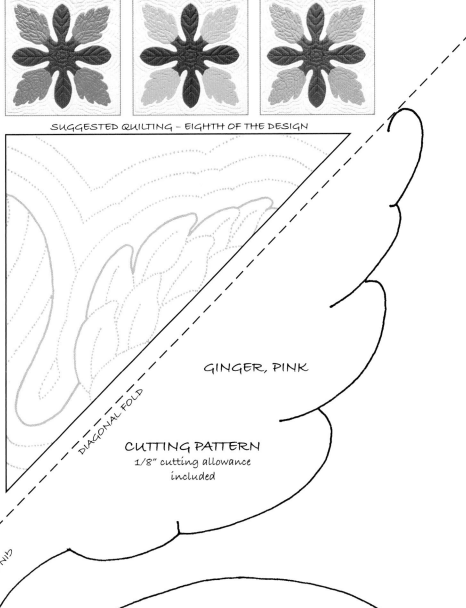

SUGGESTED QUILTING - EIGHTH OF THE DESIGN

GINGER, PINK

A delicate pink, newer variety which looks like red ginger. The sturdy, waxy pink bracts protect small delicate white flowers. It is a popular ornamental plant which is used in spectacular floral arrangements.

GINGER, PINK

DIAGONAL FOLD

CUTTING PATTERN
1/8" cutting allowance included

Companion Piece:
Heliconia,
Page 30

GINGER, PINK

© 1994 Elizabeth Root | The Pillows to Patch Quilt Collection...the Hawaiian Way

CENTER

STRAIGHT FOLD

7"

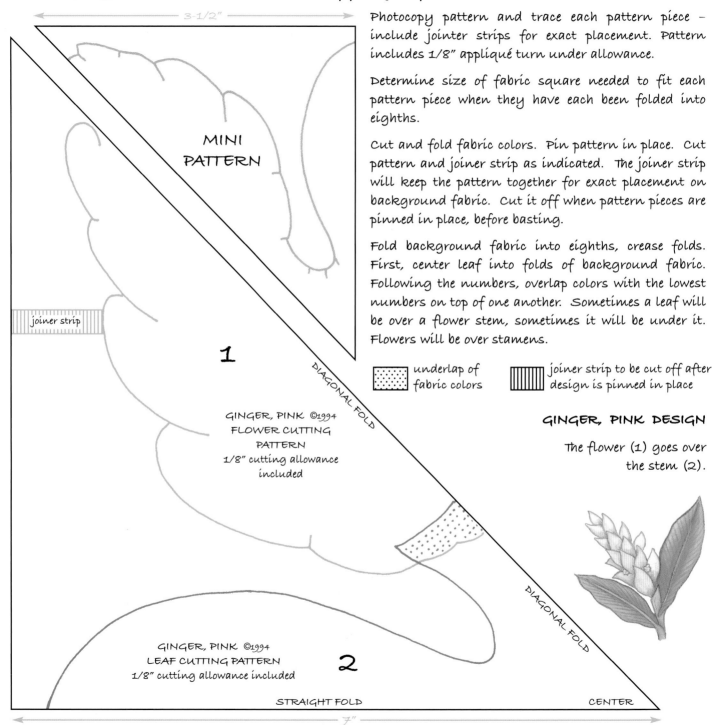

Photocopy pattern and trace each pattern piece – include jointer strips for exact placement. Pattern includes 1/8" appliqué turn under allowance.

Determine size of fabric square needed to fit each pattern piece when they have each been folded into eighths.

Cut and fold fabric colors. Pin pattern in place. Cut pattern and joiner strip as indicated. The joiner strip will keep the pattern together for exact placement on background fabric. Cut it off when pattern pieces are pinned in place, before basting.

Fold background fabric into eighths, crease folds. First, center leaf into folds of background fabric. Following the numbers, overlap colors with the lowest numbers on top of one another. Sometimes a leaf will be over a flower stem, sometimes it will be under it. Flowers will be over stamens.

underlap of fabric colors

joiner strip to be cut off after design is pinned in place

GINGER, PINK DESIGN

The flower (1) goes over the stem (2).

3-1/2"

MINI PATTERN

joiner strip

1

GINGER, PINK ©1994
FLOWER CUTTING PATTERN
1/8" cutting allowance included

DIAGONAL FOLD

DIAGONAL FOLD

GINGER, PINK ©1994
LEAF CUTTING PATTERN
1/8" cutting allowance included

2

STRAIGHT FOLD

CENTER

7"

INTERMEDIATE PATTERN

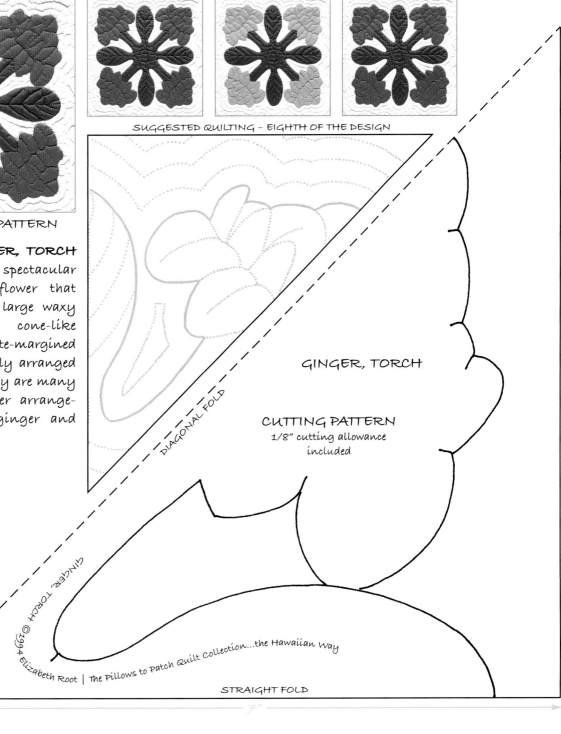

SUGGESTED QUILTING – EIGHTH OF THE DESIGN

GINGER, TORCH

A spectacular large flower that develops large waxy looking cone-like heads of white-margined bracts that are spirally arranged with tiny flowers. They are many times used in flower arrangements with pink ginger and heliconia.

GINGER, TORCH

CUTTING PATTERN
1/8" cutting allowance
included

DIAGONAL FOLD

© 1994 Elizabeth Root | The Pillows to Patch Quilt Collection...the Hawaiian Way

CENTER

STRAIGHT FOLD

GINGER, TORCH

Companion Piece:
Pikake,
Page 45

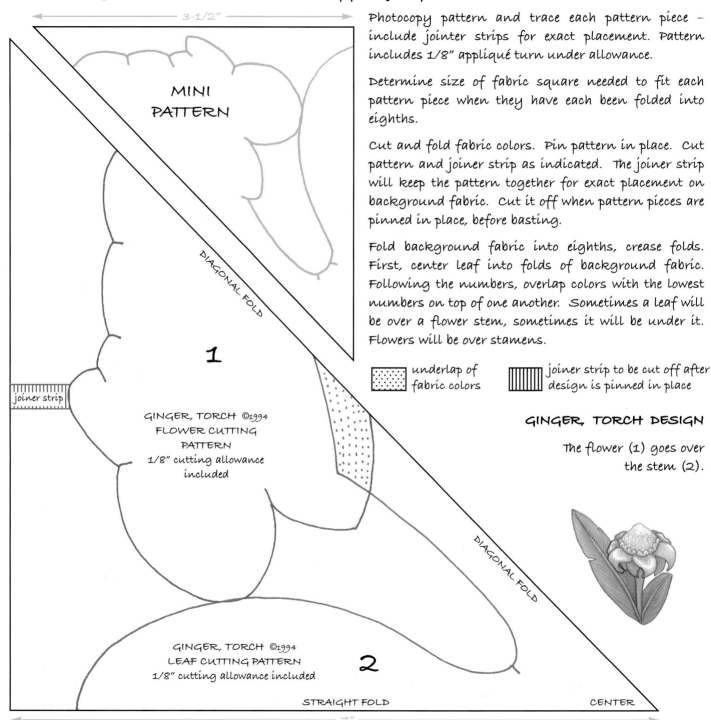

3-1/2"

MINI
PATTERN

DIAGONAL FOLD

joiner strip

1

GINGER, TORCH ©1994
FLOWER CUTTING
PATTERN
1/8" cutting allowance
included

GINGER, TORCH ©1994
LEAF CUTTING PATTERN
1/8" cutting allowance included

2

STRAIGHT FOLD

DIAGONAL FOLD

CENTER

7"

Photocopy pattern and trace each pattern piece – include jointer strips for exact placement. Pattern includes 1/8" appliqué turn under allowance.

Determine size of fabric square needed to fit each pattern piece when they have each been folded into eighths.

Cut and fold fabric colors. Pin pattern in place. Cut pattern and joiner strip as indicated. The joiner strip will keep the pattern together for exact placement on background fabric. Cut it off when pattern pieces are pinned in place, before basting.

Fold background fabric into eighths, crease folds. First, center leaf into folds of background fabric. Following the numbers, overlap colors with the lowest numbers on top of one another. Sometimes a leaf will be over a flower stem, sometimes it will be under it. Flowers will be over stamens.

underlap of fabric colors

joiner strip to be cut off after design is pinned in place

GINGER, TORCH DESIGN

The flower (1) goes over the stem (2).

ADVANCED PATTERN

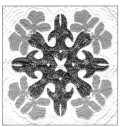

SUGGESTED QUILTING – EIGHTH OF THE DESIGN

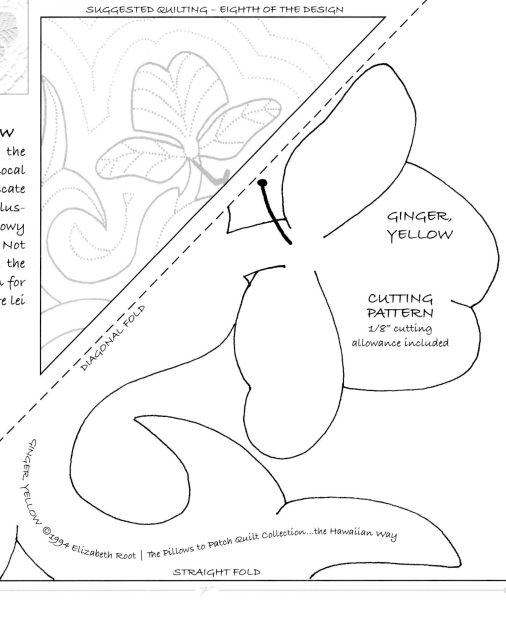

GINGER, YELLOW

Found along the roadside and in local gardens – its delicate yellow blossoms cluster together in a showy head of flowers. Not unlike its white counterpart, the yellow ginger is better known for its intense fragrance. Both are lei flowers for special occasions.

GINGER, YELLOW

CUTTING PATTERN
1/8" cutting allowance included

DIAGONAL FOLD

GINGER, YELLOW ©1994 Elizabeth Root | The Pillows to Patch Quilt Collection...the Hawaiian Way

CENTER

STRAIGHT FOLD

7"

Companion Piece:
Orchid,
Page 42

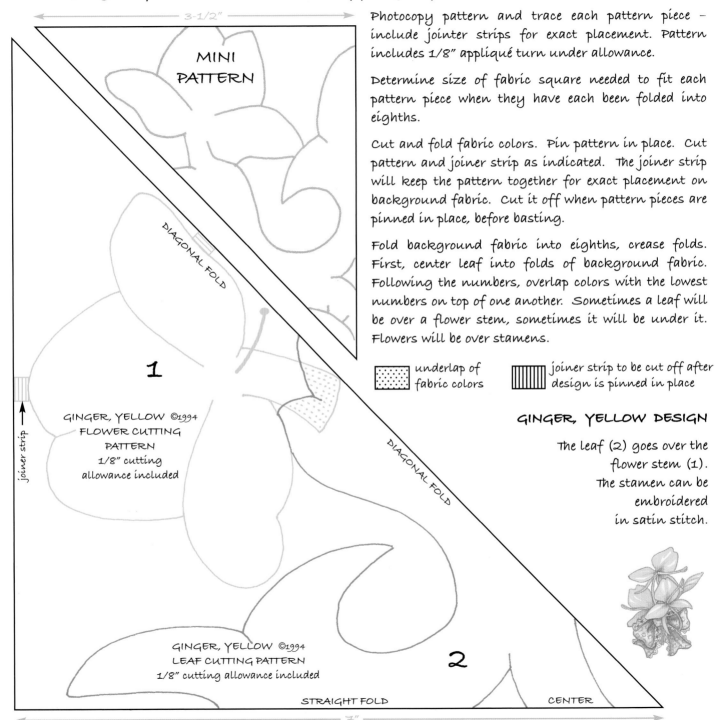

3-1/2"

MINI PATTERN

DIAGONAL FOLD

1

joiner strip

GINGER, YELLOW ©1994
FLOWER CUTTING
PATTERN
1/8" cutting
allowance included

DIAGONAL FOLD

GINGER, YELLOW ©1994
LEAF CUTTING PATTERN
1/8" cutting allowance included

2

STRAIGHT FOLD

CENTER

7"

Photocopy pattern and trace each pattern piece – include joiner strips for exact placement. Pattern includes 1/8" appliqué turn under allowance.

Determine size of fabric square needed to fit each pattern piece when they have each been folded into eighths.

Cut and fold fabric colors. Pin pattern in place. Cut pattern and joiner strip as indicated. The joiner strip will keep the pattern together for exact placement on background fabric. Cut it off when pattern pieces are pinned in place, before basting.

Fold background fabric into eighths, crease folds. First, center leaf into folds of background fabric. Following the numbers, overlap colors with the lowest numbers on top of one another. Sometimes a leaf will be over a flower stem, sometimes it will be under it. Flowers will be over stamens.

underlap of fabric colors

joiner strip to be cut off after design is pinned in place

GINGER, YELLOW DESIGN

The leaf (2) goes over the
flower stem (1).
The stamen can be
embroidered
in satin stitch.

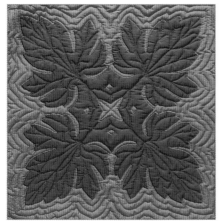

INTERMEDIATE PATTERN

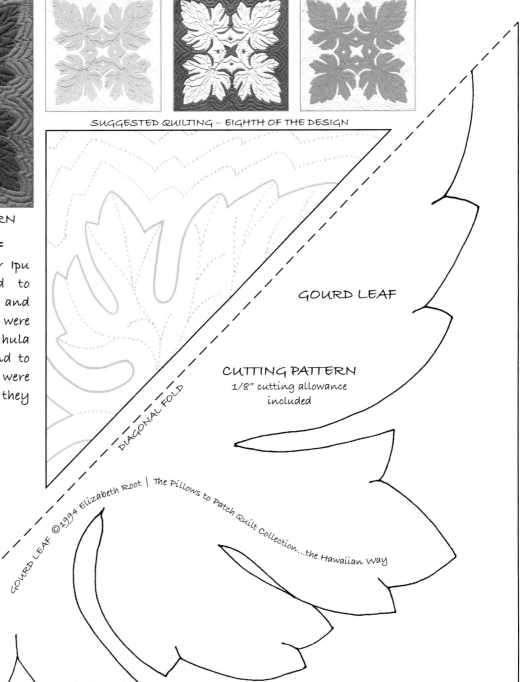

SUGGESTED QUILTING – EIGHTH OF THE DESIGN

GOURD LEAF

Gourds or Ipu were used to hold food and water. They were also used in hula as instruments, drums, and to hold tapa cloth. Some were decorated with designs as they still are today.

GOURD LEAF

CUTTING PATTERN
1/8" cutting allowance
included

DIAGONAL FOLD

GOURD LEAF ©1994 Elizabeth Root | The Pillows to Patch Quilt Collection...the Hawaiian Way

Companion Piece:
Papaya Leaf,
Page 44

CENTER   STRAIGHT FOLD

7"

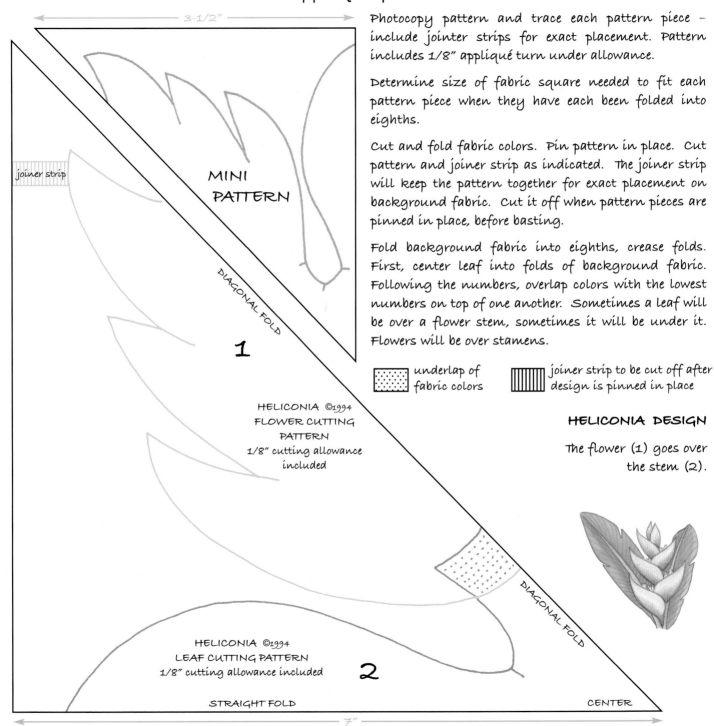

3-1/2"

joiner strip

MINI
PATTERN

DIAGONAL FOLD

1

HELICONIA ©1994
FLOWER CUTTING
PATTERN
1/8" cutting allowance
included

DIAGONAL FOLD

HELICONIA ©1994
LEAF CUTTING PATTERN
1/8" cutting allowance included

2

STRAIGHT FOLD

CENTER

7"

Photocopy pattern and trace each pattern piece – include jointer strips for exact placement. Pattern includes 1/8" appliqué turn under allowance.

Determine size of fabric square needed to fit each pattern piece when they have each been folded into eighths.

Cut and fold fabric colors. Pin pattern in place. Cut pattern and joiner strip as indicated. The joiner strip will keep the pattern together for exact placement on background fabric. Cut it off when pattern pieces are pinned in place, before basting.

Fold background fabric into eighths, crease folds. First, center leaf into folds of background fabric. Following the numbers, overlap colors with the lowest numbers on top of one another. Sometimes a leaf will be over a flower stem, sometimes it will be under it. Flowers will be over stamens.

underlap of fabric colors

joiner strip to be cut off after design is pinned in place

HELICONIA DESIGN

The flower (1) goes over the stem (2).

INTERMEDIATE PATTERN

SUGGESTED QUILTING – EIGHTH OF THE DESIGN

HELICONIA

Named for Mount Helicon in Greece, these unique flowers are used in spectacular flower arrangements. Sometimes called "false bird of paradise," in Hawaii the most common variety is the red large bract variety also called "lobster claw."

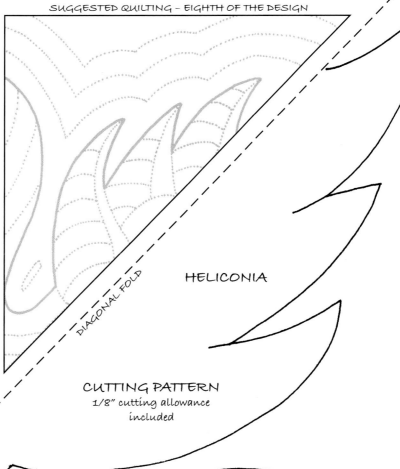

DIAGONAL FOLD

HELICONIA

CUTTING PATTERN
1/8" cutting allowance included

Companion Piece:
Ginger, Pink,
Page 23

HELICONIA ©1994 Elizabeth Root | The Pillows to Patch Quilt Collection...the Hawaiian Way

CENTER   STRAIGHT FOLD

7"

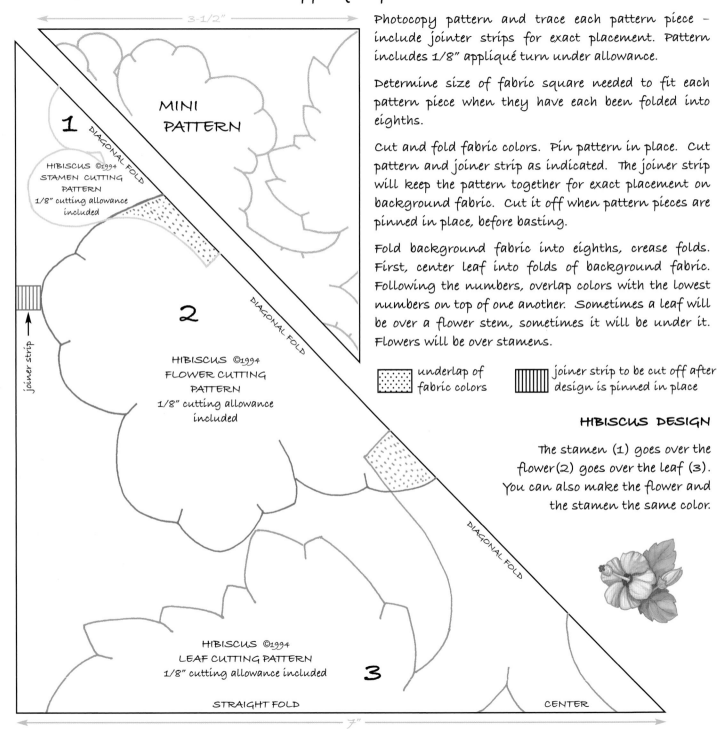

3-1/2"

DIAGONAL FOLD

MINI
PATTERN

1

HIBISCUS ©1994
STAMEN CUTTING
PATTERN
1/8" cutting allowance
included

joiner strip

2

HIBISCUS ©1994
FLOWER CUTTING
PATTERN
1/8" cutting allowance
included

DIAGONAL FOLD

DIAGONAL FOLD

3

HIBISCUS ©1994
LEAF CUTTING PATTERN
1/8" cutting allowance included

STRAIGHT FOLD

CENTER

7"

Photocopy pattern and trace each pattern piece – include jointer strips for exact placement. Pattern includes 1/8" appliqué turn under allowance.

Determine size of fabric square needed to fit each pattern piece when they have each been folded into eighths.

Cut and fold fabric colors. Pin pattern in place. Cut pattern and joiner strip as indicated. The joiner strip will keep the pattern together for exact placement on background fabric. Cut it off when pattern pieces are pinned in place, before basting.

Fold background fabric into eighths, crease folds. First, center leaf into folds of background fabric. Following the numbers, overlap colors with the lowest numbers on top of one another. Sometimes a leaf will be over a flower stem, sometimes it will be under it. Flowers will be over stamens.

underlap of fabric colors

joiner strip to be cut off after design is pinned in place

HIBISCUS DESIGN

The stamen (1) goes over the flower (2) goes over the leaf (3). You can also make the flower and the stamen the same color.

INTERMEDIATE PATTERN

HIBISCUS

Hawaii's State Flower - myriad varieties can be seen throughout Hawaii. Picked, it can last one day without water, closing a night to open, renewed for another day's beauty.

Companion Piece: Chrysanthemum, Page 16

SUGGESTED QUILTING – EIGHTH OF THE DESIGN

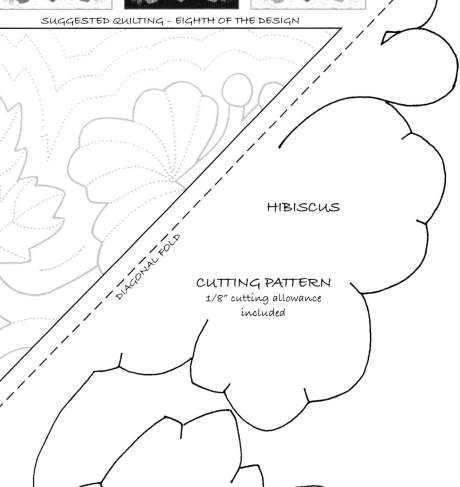

DIAGONAL FOLD

HIBISCUS

CUTTING PATTERN
1/8" cutting allowance included

HIBISCUS ©1994 Elizabeth Root | The Pillows to Patch Quilt Collection...the Hawaiian Way

CENTER

STRAIGHT FOLD

7"

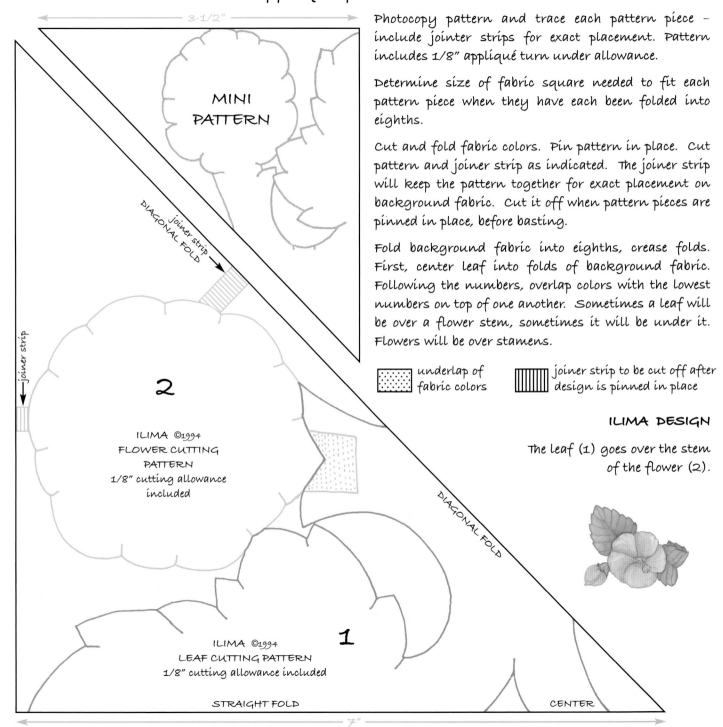

3-1/2"

MINI PATTERN

DIAGONAL FOLD

Joiner strip

joiner strip

2

ILIMA ©1994
FLOWER CUTTING
PATTERN
1/8" cutting allowance
included

DIAGONAL FOLD

1

ILIMA ©1994
LEAF CUTTING PATTERN
1/8" cutting allowance included

STRAIGHT FOLD

CENTER

7"

Photocopy pattern and trace each pattern piece – include jointer strips for exact placement. Pattern includes 1/8" appliqué turn under allowance.

Determine size of fabric square needed to fit each pattern piece when they have each been folded into eighths.

Cut and fold fabric colors. Pin pattern in place. Cut pattern and joiner strip as indicated. The joiner strip will keep the pattern together for exact placement on background fabric. Cut it off when pattern pieces are pinned in place, before basting.

Fold background fabric into eighths, crease folds. First, center leaf into folds of background fabric. Following the numbers, overlap colors with the lowest numbers on top of one another. Sometimes a leaf will be over a flower stem, sometimes it will be under it. Flowers will be over stamens.

[dotted icon] underlap of fabric colors

[striped icon] joiner strip to be cut off after design is pinned in place

ILIMA DESIGN

The leaf (1) goes over the stem of the flower (2).

ADVANCED PATTERN

ILIMA

The flower of Oahu, the flowers are cultivated for leis. Commonly entwined with the sweet-smelling maile leaf, and worn at state occasions. Laka, the goddess of hula, could take the ilima flower form at will.

Companion Piece:
Plumeria,
Page 47

SUGGESTED QUILTING – EIGHTH OF THE DESIGN

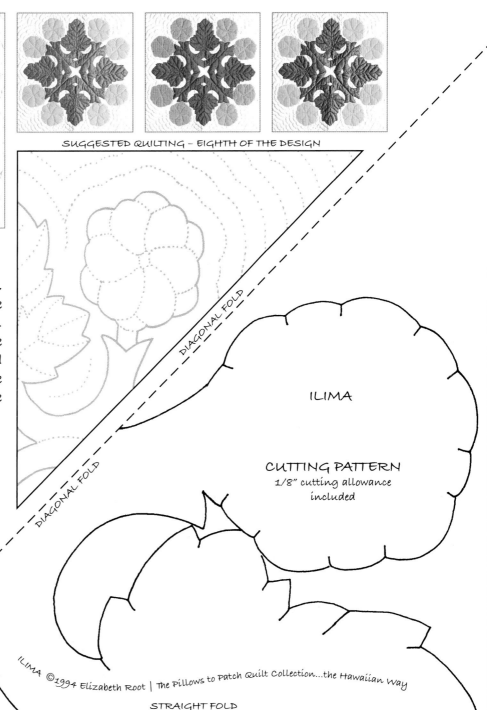

DIAGONAL FOLD

DIAGONAL FOLD

ILIMA

CUTTING PATTERN
1/8" cutting allowance
included

ILIMA ©1994 Elizabeth Root | The Pillows to Patch Quilt Collection...the Hawaiian Way

CENTER

STRAIGHT FOLD

7"

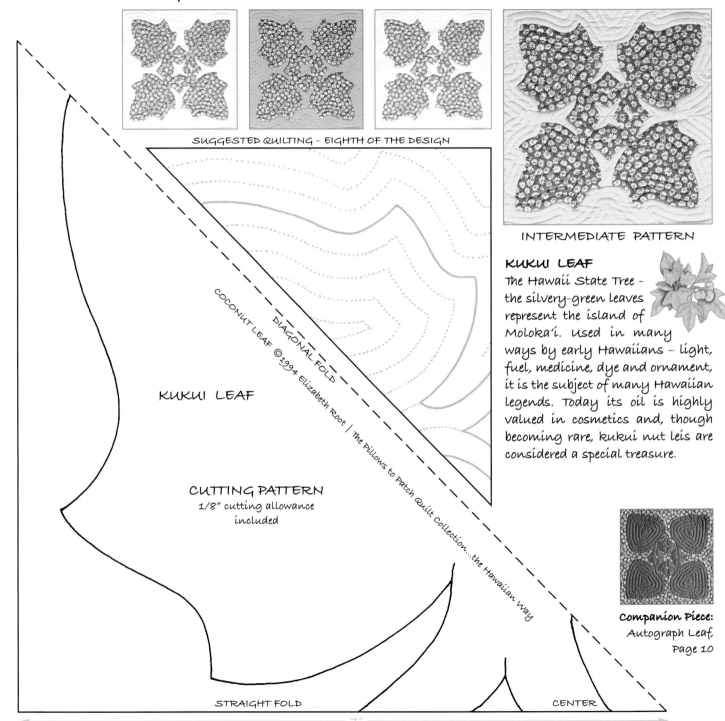

SUGGESTED QUILTING - EIGHTH OF THE DESIGN

INTERMEDIATE PATTERN

DIAGONAL FOLD

COCONUT LEAF ©1994 Elizabeth Root | The Pillows to Patch Quilt Collection...the Hawaiian Way

KUKUI LEAF

CUTTING PATTERN
1/8" cutting allowance
included

KUKUI LEAF

The Hawaii State Tree – the silvery-green leaves represent the island of Moloka'i. Used in many ways by early Hawaiians – light, fuel, medicine, dye and ornament, it is the subject of many Hawaiian legends. Today its oil is highly valued in cosmetics and, though becoming rare, kukui nut leis are considered a special treasure.

Companion Piece:
Autograph Leaf,
Page 10

STRAIGHT FOLD

CENTER

7"

ADVANCED PATTERN

LEHUA

The delicate, flower of Hawaii island, is conspicuous because of its myriad stamens forming a fuzzy mound. Usually red, matching the bright plumage of the small 'i'iwi bird that thrives on its honey. The lehua is the subject of many legends — it is said that if a lehua flower is picked on the way to the mountains, it will rain.

Companion Piece:
Carnation,
Page 14

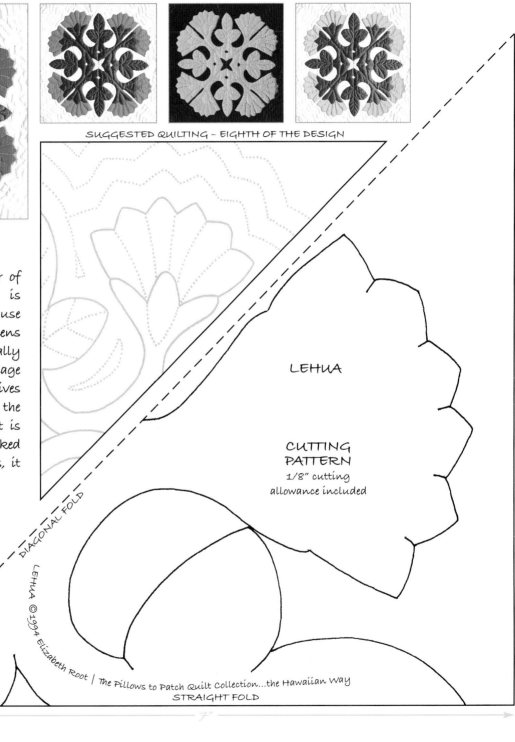

SUGGESTED QUILTING – EIGHTH OF THE DESIGN

DIAGONAL FOLD

LEHUA © 1994 Elizabeth Root | The Pillows to Patch Quilt Collection...the Hawaiian Way

LEHUA

CUTTING
PATTERN
1/8" cutting
allowance included

CENTER

STRAIGHT FOLD

7"

38 Lehua – multicolor appliqué pattern

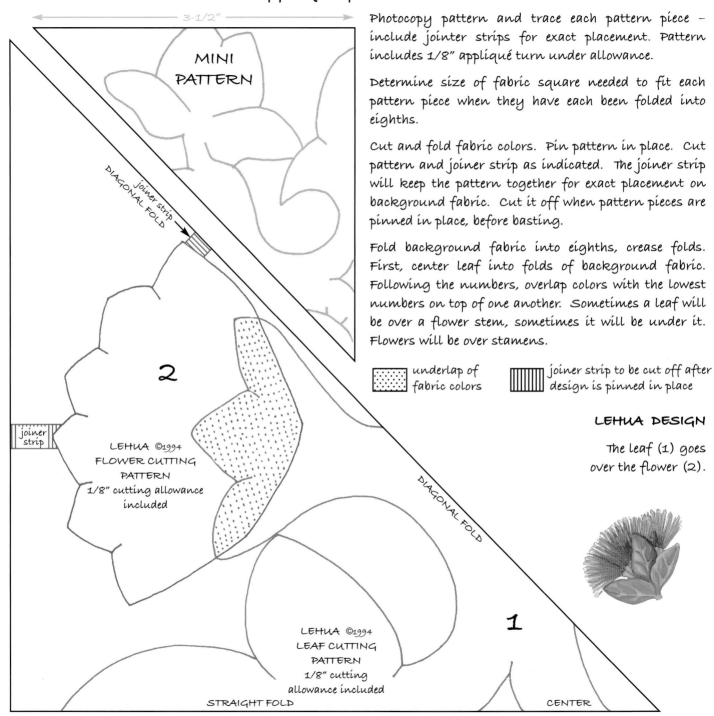

3-1/2"

MINI
PATTERN

joiner strip

DIAGONAL FOLD

2

joiner strip

LEHUA ©1994
FLOWER CUTTING
PATTERN
1/8" cutting allowance
included

DIAGONAL FOLD

1

LEHUA ©1994
LEAF CUTTING
PATTERN
1/8" cutting
allowance included

STRAIGHT FOLD

CENTER

7"

Photocopy pattern and trace each pattern piece – include jointer strips for exact placement. Pattern includes 1/8" appliqué turn under allowance.

Determine size of fabric square needed to fit each pattern piece when they have each been folded into eighths.

Cut and fold fabric colors. Pin pattern in place. Cut pattern and joiner strip as indicated. The joiner strip will keep the pattern together for exact placement on background fabric. Cut it off when pattern pieces are pinned in place, before basting.

Fold background fabric into eighths, crease folds. First, center leaf into folds of background fabric. Following the numbers, overlap colors with the lowest numbers on top of one another. Sometimes a leaf will be over a flower stem, sometimes it will be under it. Flowers will be over stamens.

underlap of fabric colors

joiner strip to be cut off after design is pinned in place

LEHUA DESIGN

The leaf (1) goes
over the flower (2).

INTERMEDIATE PATTERN

LOKELANI ROSE

The double pink rose which is the flower of the island of Maui is, today, rarely found.

Roses have always been popular in Hawaii. Queen Emma was proud of her garden at her summer palace in Nuuanu on Oahu.

Companion Piece:
Crown Flower,
Page 19

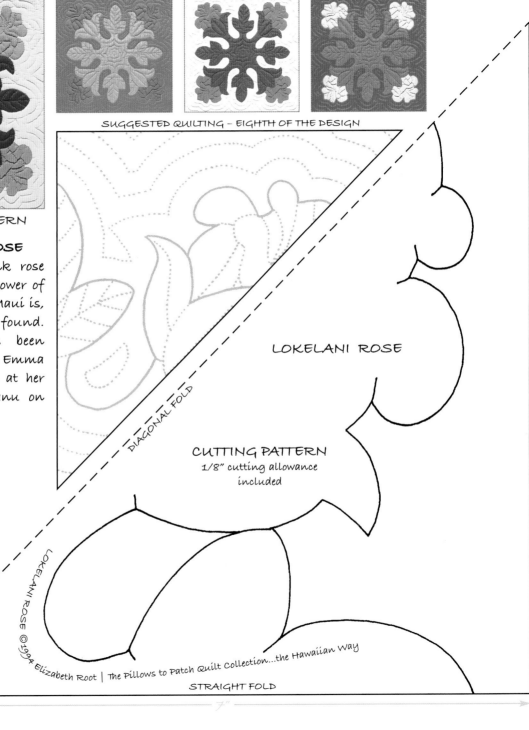

SUGGESTED QUILTING – EIGHTH OF THE DESIGN

LOKELANI ROSE

DIAGONAL FOLD

CUTTING PATTERN
1/8" cutting allowance
included

LOKELANI ROSE © 1994 Elizabeth Root | The Pillows to Patch Quilt Collection...the Hawaiian Way

CENTER

STRAIGHT FOLD

7"

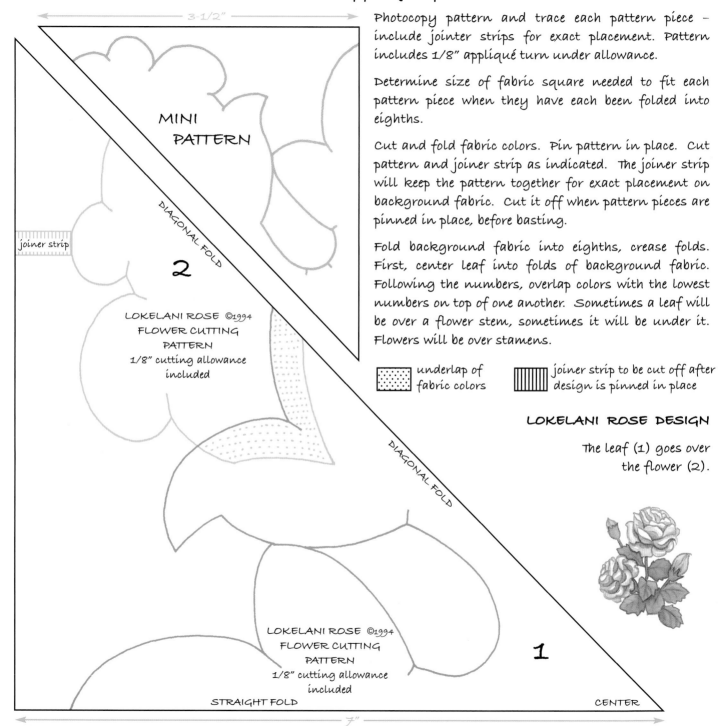

3-1/2"

MINI
PATTERN

DIAGONAL FOLD

joiner strip

2

LOKELANI ROSE ©1994
FLOWER CUTTING
PATTERN
1/8" cutting allowance
included

DIAGONAL FOLD

LOKELANI ROSE ©1994
FLOWER CUTTING
PATTERN
1/8" cutting allowance
included

STRAIGHT FOLD

1

CENTER

7"

Photocopy pattern and trace each pattern piece – include jointer strips for exact placement. Pattern includes 1/8" appliqué turn under allowance.

Determine size of fabric square needed to fit each pattern piece when they have each been folded into eighths.

Cut and fold fabric colors. Pin pattern in place. Cut pattern and joiner strip as indicated. The joiner strip will keep the pattern together for exact placement on background fabric. Cut it off when pattern pieces are pinned in place, before basting.

Fold background fabric into eighths, crease folds. First, center leaf into folds of background fabric. Following the numbers, overlap colors with the lowest numbers on top of one another. Sometimes a leaf will be over a flower stem, sometimes it will be under it. Flowers will be over stamens.

▒ underlap of
  fabric colors

▥ joiner strip to be cut off after
  design is pinned in place

LOKELANI ROSE DESIGN

The leaf (1) goes over
the flower (2).

INTERMEDIATE PATTERN

MONSTERA LEAF

Part of the Taro vine family, this large, impressive leaf - up to 3 feet long - can be seen growing throughout the trees on thick vines. It has an edible fruit that tastes like a mixture of pineapple and banana.

SUGGESTED QUILTING – EIGHTH OF THE DESIGN

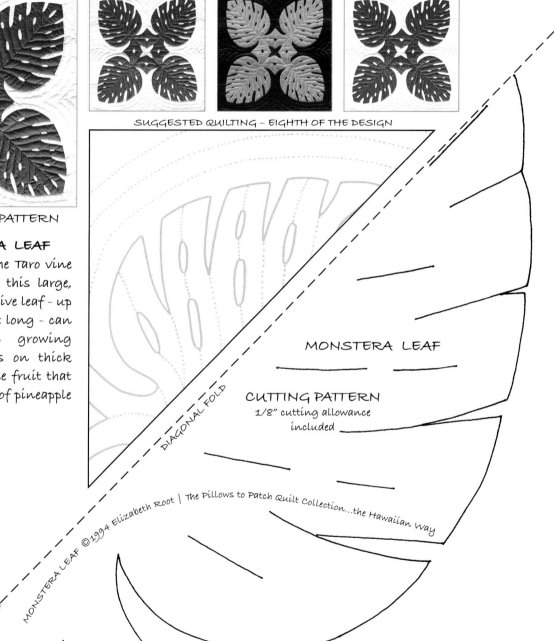

MONSTERA LEAF

CUTTING PATTERN
1/8" cutting allowance
included

DIAGONAL FOLD

MONSTERA LEAF ©1994 Elizabeth Root | The Pillows to Patch Quilt Collection...the Hawaiian Way

CENTER   STRAIGHT FOLD

7"

Companion Piece:
Papaya Leaf,
Page 44

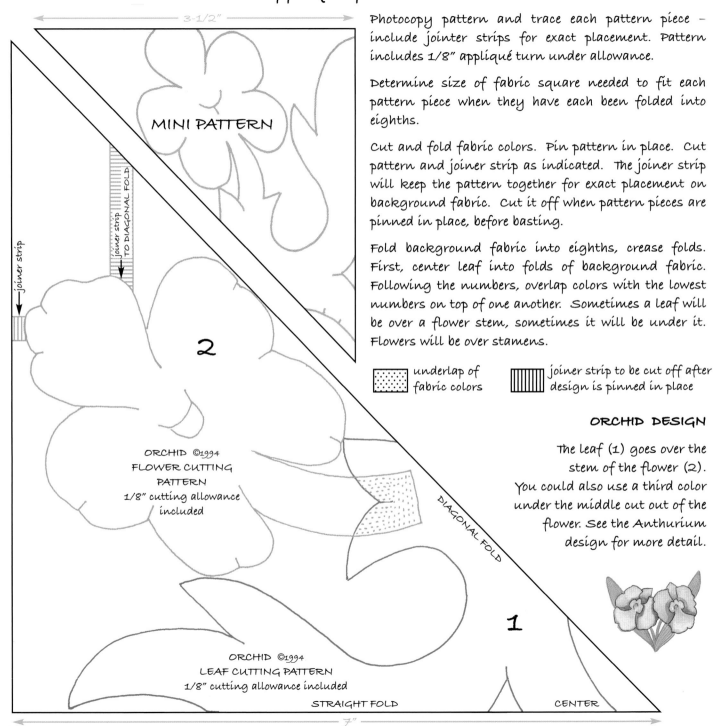

3-1/2"

MINI PATTERN

joiner strip TO DIAGONAL FOLD

joiner strip

2

ORCHID ©1994
FLOWER CUTTING
PATTERN
1/8" cutting allowance
included

DIAGONAL FOLD

1

ORCHID ©1994
LEAF CUTTING PATTERN
1/8" cutting allowance included

STRAIGHT FOLD   CENTER

7"

Photocopy pattern and trace each pattern piece – include jointer strips for exact placement. Pattern includes 1/8" appliqué turn under allowance.

Determine size of fabric square needed to fit each pattern piece when they have each been folded into eighths.

Cut and fold fabric colors. Pin pattern in place. Cut pattern and joiner strip as indicated. The joiner strip will keep the pattern together for exact placement on background fabric. Cut it off when pattern pieces are pinned in place, before basting.

Fold background fabric into eighths, crease folds. First, center leaf into folds of background fabric. Following the numbers, overlap colors with the lowest numbers on top of one another. Sometimes a leaf will be over a flower stem, sometimes it will be under it. Flowers will be over stamens.

underlap of fabric colors

joiner strip to be cut off after design is pinned in place

ORCHID DESIGN

The leaf (1) goes over the stem of the flower (2). You could also use a third color under the middle cut out of the flower. See the Anthurium design for more detail.

ADVANCED PATTERN

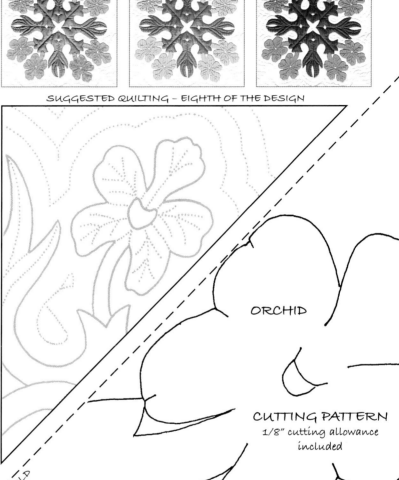

SUGGESTED QUILTING – EIGHTH OF THE DESIGN

ORCHID
Growing wild in the ferns up mountainsides, cultivated in private gardens for enjoyment and show, grown commercially as plants and flowers, worn daily as leis - the hundreds of varieties of orchid enjoy Hawaii's climate and adulation.

ORCHID

CUTTING PATTERN
1/8" cutting allowance
included

DIAGONAL FOLD

Companion Piece:
Yellow Ginger,
Page 27

ORCHID ©1994 Elizabeth Root | The Pillows to Patch Quilt Collection...the Hawaiian Way

CENTER

STRAIGHT FOLD

7"

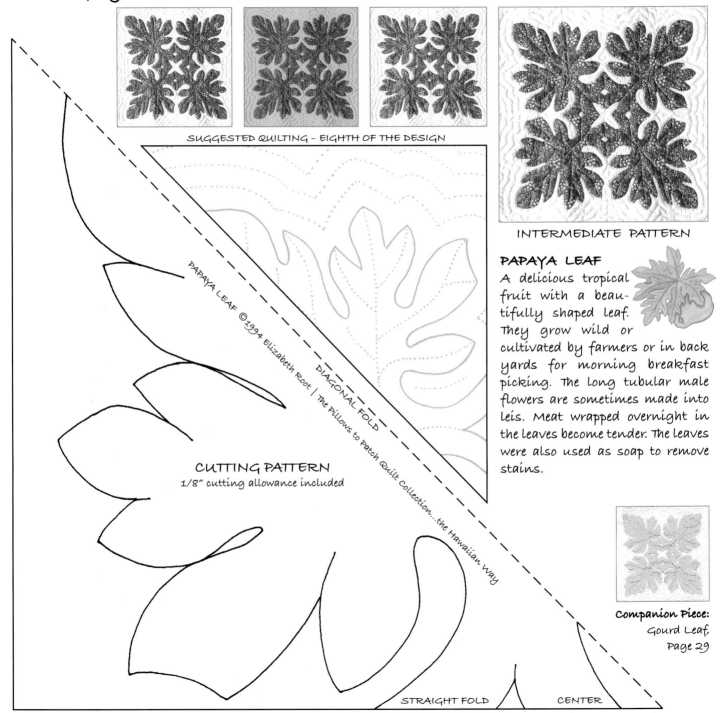

SUGGESTED QUILTING – EIGHTH OF THE DESIGN

INTERMEDIATE PATTERN

PAPAYA LEAF ©1994 Elizabeth Root | The Pillows to Patch Quilt Collection...the Hawaiian Way

DIAGONAL FOLD

CUTTING PATTERN
1/8" cutting allowance included

STRAIGHT FOLD

CENTER

7"

PAPAYA LEAF
A delicious tropical fruit with a beautifully shaped leaf. They grow wild or cultivated by farmers or in back yards for morning breakfast picking. The long tubular male flowers are sometimes made into leis. Meat wrapped overnight in the leaves become tender. The leaves were also used as soap to remove stains.

Companion Piece:
Gourd Leaf,
Page 29

INTERMEDIATE PATTERN

PIKAKE

For some unknown reason the flower was so named be-cause of Princess Kaiulani's fondness for this white fragrant blossom and the peacock. These blossoms, pearl-like when closed and rose-like when open, are a special lei flower with a scent that, at any age, brings back fond memories when wearing a pikake lei.

Companion Piece: Ginger, Torch, Page 25

SUGGESTED QUILTING – EIGHTH OF THE DESIGN

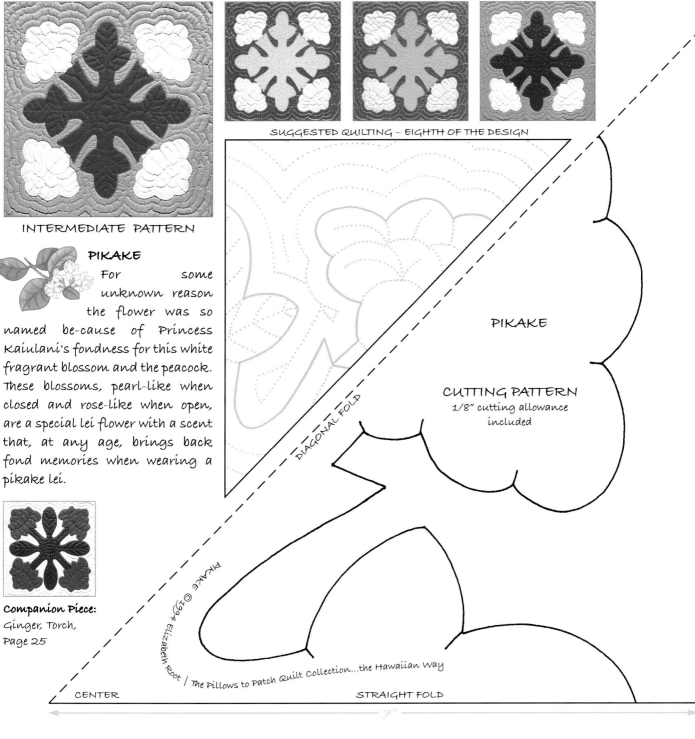

PIKAKE

CUTTING PATTERN
1/8" cutting allowance included

DIAGONAL FOLD

PIKAKE © 1994 Elizabeth Root / The Pillows to Patch Quilt Collection...the Hawaiian Way

CENTER

STRAIGHT FOLD

7"

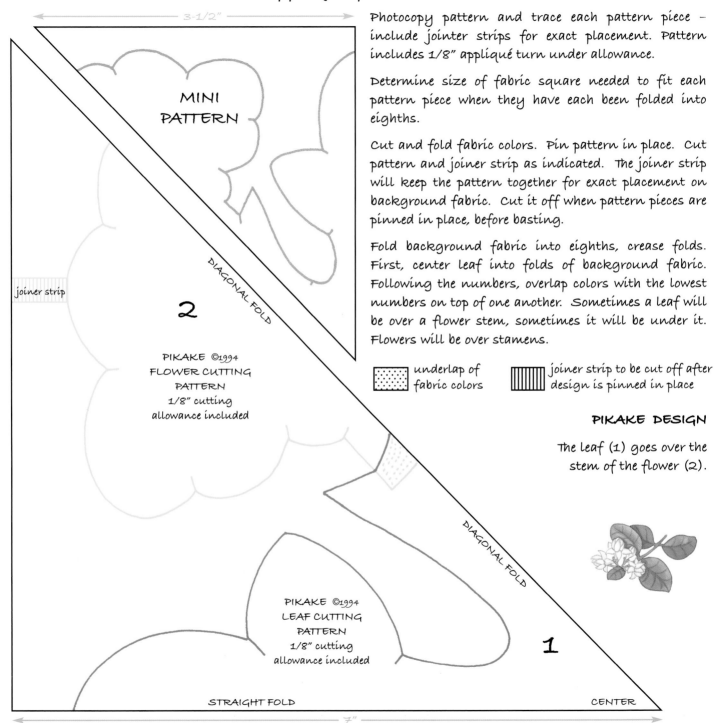

3-1/2"

MINI
PATTERN

joiner strip

2

PIKAKE ©1994
FLOWER CUTTING
PATTERN
1/8" cutting
allowance included

DIAGONAL FOLD

DIAGONAL FOLD

1

PIKAKE ©1994
LEAF CUTTING
PATTERN
1/8" cutting
allowance included

STRAIGHT FOLD

CENTER

7"

Photocopy pattern and trace each pattern piece – include jointer strips for exact placement. Pattern includes 1/8" appliqué turn under allowance.

Determine size of fabric square needed to fit each pattern piece when they have each been folded into eighths.

Cut and fold fabric colors. Pin pattern in place. Cut pattern and joiner strip as indicated. The joiner strip will keep the pattern together for exact placement on background fabric. Cut it off when pattern pieces are pinned in place, before basting.

Fold background fabric into eighths, crease folds. First, center leaf into folds of background fabric. Following the numbers, overlap colors with the lowest numbers on top of one another. Sometimes a leaf will be over a flower stem, sometimes it will be under it. Flowers will be over stamens.

underlap of fabric colors

joiner strip to be cut off after design is pinned in place

PIKAKE DESIGN

The leaf (1) goes over the stem of the flower (2).

ADVANCED PATTERN

PLUMERIA

These waxy flowers, white to rainbow, fragrance Hawaii's islands. Grown in backyards, seen along roadsides or cultivated in flower farms – it is a favorite lei flower.

Companion Piece:
Ilima,
Page 34

SUGGESTED QUILTING – EIGHTH OF THE DESIGN

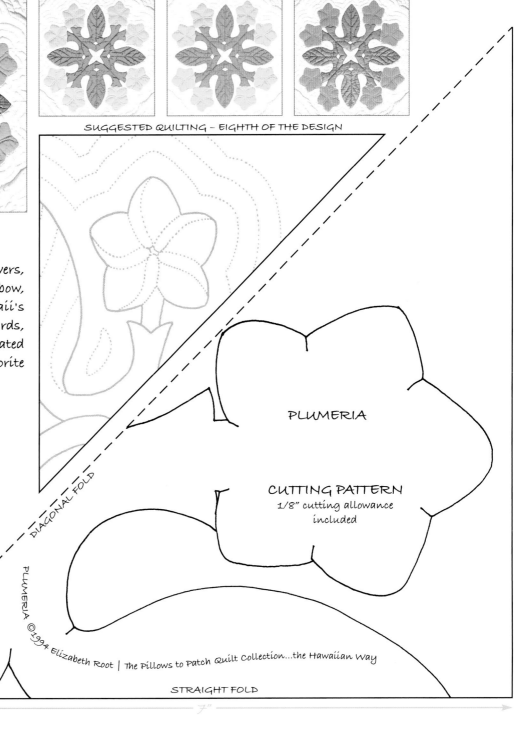

PLUMERIA

CUTTING PATTERN
1/8" cutting allowance
included

DIAGONAL FOLD

PLUMERIA

PLUMERIA ©1994 Elizabeth Root | The Pillows to Patch Quilt Collection...the Hawaiian Way

CENTER

STRAIGHT FOLD

7"

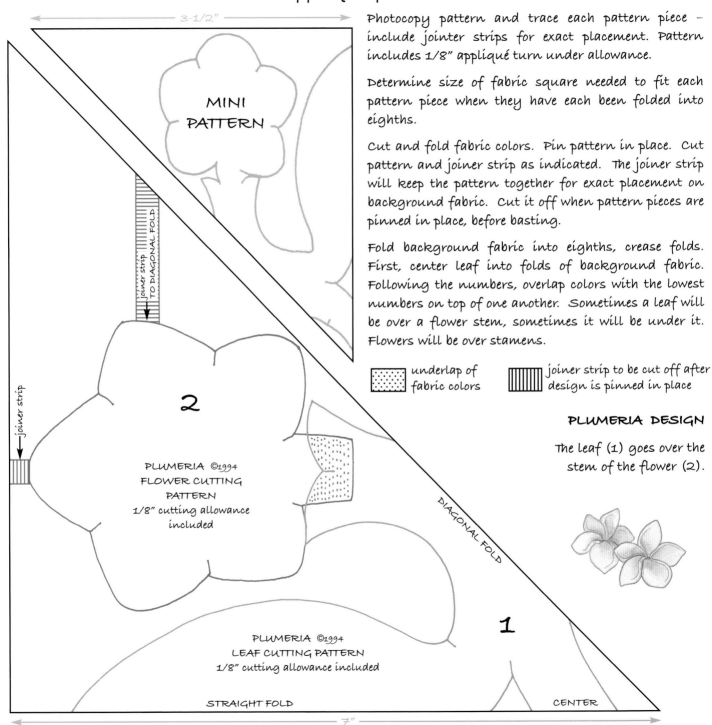

3-1/2"

MINI PATTERN

joiner strip — TO DIAGONAL FOLD

joiner strip

2

PLUMERIA ©1994
FLOWER CUTTING
PATTERN
1/8" cutting allowance
included

DIAGONAL FOLD

1

PLUMERIA ©1994
LEAF CUTTING PATTERN
1/8" cutting allowance included

STRAIGHT FOLD

CENTER

7"

Photocopy pattern and trace each pattern piece – include jointer strips for exact placement. Pattern includes 1/8" appliqué turn under allowance.

Determine size of fabric square needed to fit each pattern piece when they have each been folded into eighths.

Cut and fold fabric colors. Pin pattern in place. Cut pattern and joiner strip as indicated. The joiner strip will keep the pattern together for exact placement on background fabric. Cut it off when pattern pieces are pinned in place, before basting.

Fold background fabric into eighths, crease folds. First, center leaf into folds of background fabric. Following the numbers, overlap colors with the lowest numbers on top of one another. Sometimes a leaf will be over a flower stem, sometimes it will be under it. Flowers will be over stamens.

underlap of fabric colors

joiner strip to be cut off after design is pinned in place

PLUMERIA DESIGN

The leaf (1) goes over the stem of the flower (2).

ADVANCED PATTERN

PROTEA FAN DANCER

Spectacular pink feather-like petals, tipped with black fuzz. Reminiscent of dancing girls' large, showy fans. Used in floral arrangements and wreaths that dry naturally.

SUGGESTED QUILTING – EIGHTH OF THE DESIGN

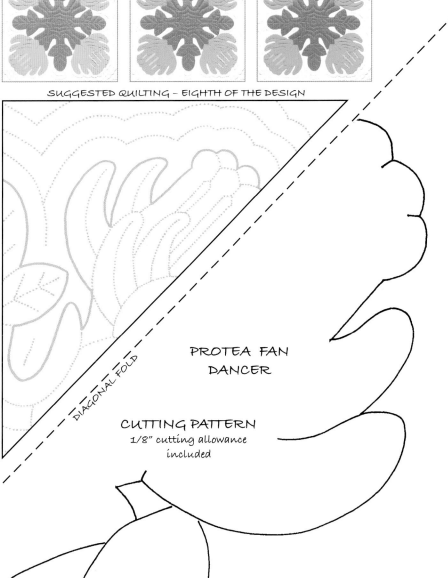

DIAGONAL FOLD

PROTEA FAN DANCER

CUTTING PATTERN
1/8" cutting allowance included

PROTEA FAN DANCER ©1994 Elizabeth Root | The Pillows to Patch Quilt Collection...the Hawaiian Way

Companion Piece:
Protea Queen,
Page 51

CENTER

STRAIGHT FOLD

7"

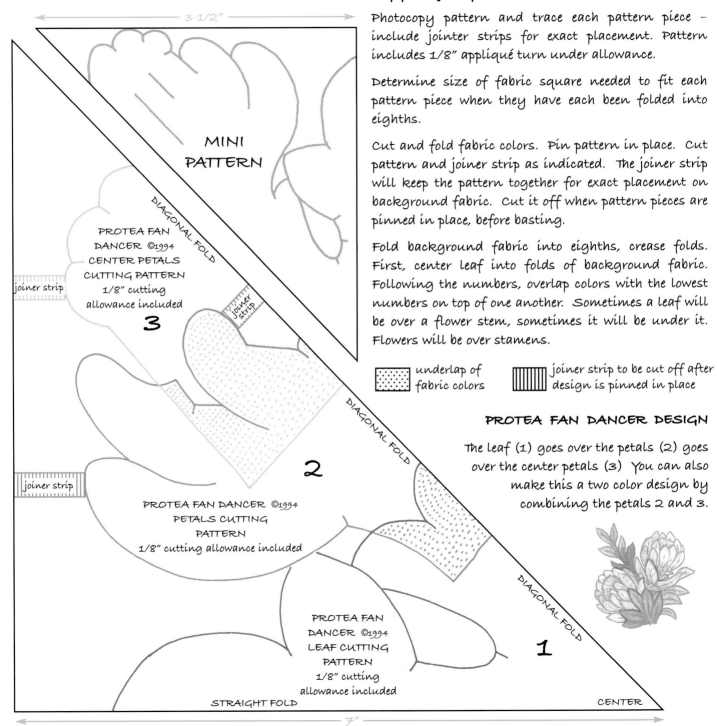

Photocopy pattern and trace each pattern piece – include jointer strips for exact placement. Pattern includes 1/8" appliqué turn under allowance.

Determine size of fabric square needed to fit each pattern piece when they have each been folded into eighths.

Cut and fold fabric colors. Pin pattern in place. Cut pattern and joiner strip as indicated. The joiner strip will keep the pattern together for exact placement on background fabric. Cut it off when pattern pieces are pinned in place, before basting.

Fold background fabric into eighths, crease folds. First, center leaf into folds of background fabric. Following the numbers, overlap colors with the lowest numbers on top of one another. Sometimes a leaf will be over a flower stem, sometimes it will be under it. Flowers will be over stamens.

underlap of fabric colors

joiner strip to be cut off after design is pinned in place

PROTEA FAN DANCER DESIGN

The leaf (1) goes over the petals (2) goes over the center petals (3) You can also make this a two color design by combining the petals 2 and 3.

MINI PATTERN

3-1/2"

DIAGONAL FOLD

joiner strip

PROTEA FAN DANCER ©1994 CENTER PETALS CUTTING PATTERN 1/8" cutting allowance included

3

joiner strip

DIAGONAL FOLD

joiner strip

2

PROTEA FAN DANCER ©1994 PETALS CUTTING PATTERN 1/8" cutting allowance included

PROTEA FAN DANCER ©1994 LEAF CUTTING PATTERN 1/8" cutting allowance included

1

DIAGONAL FOLD

STRAIGHT FOLD

CENTER

7"

ADVANCED PATTERN

PROTEA QUEEN

The larger of the myriad varieties in the protea family. Used as a focal point in arrangements, its soft downy dome, smooth to the touch like the fine fur or feathers trimming a queen's royal robes.

Companion Piece:
Protea Fan Dancer,
Page 49

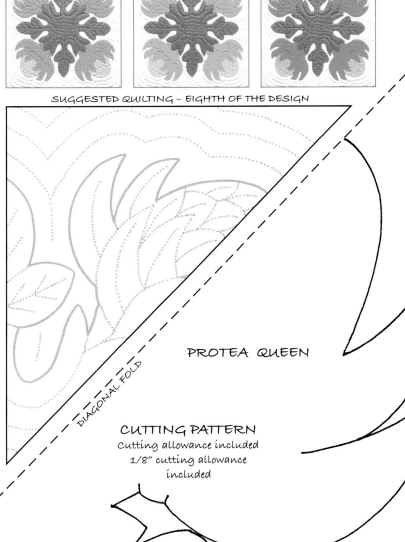

SUGGESTED QUILTING – EIGHTH OF THE DESIGN

PROTEA QUEEN

DIAGONAL FOLD

CUTTING PATTERN
Cutting allowance included
1/8" cutting allowance
included

PROTEA QUEEN

©1994 Elizabeth Root | The Pillows to Patch Quilt Collection...the Hawaiian Way

CENTER   STRAIGHT FOLD

7"

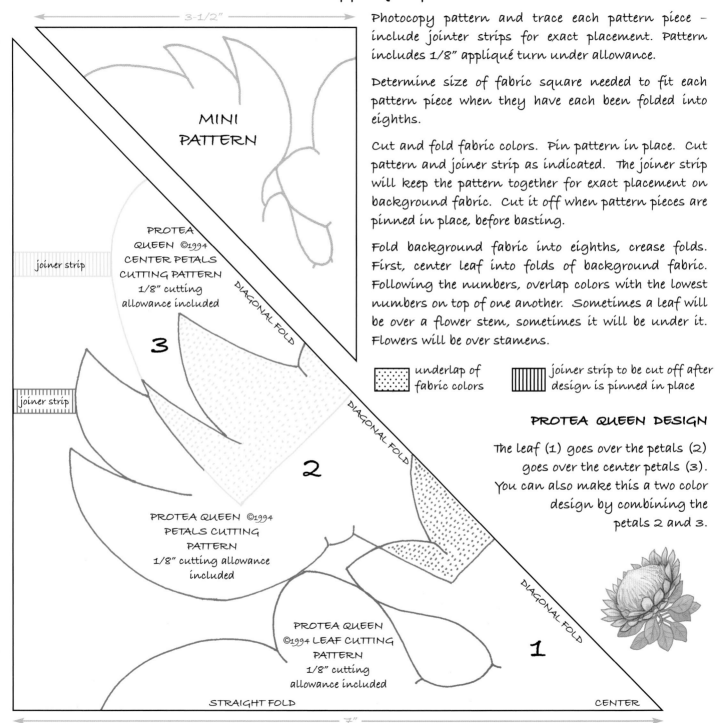

3-1/2"

MINI PATTERN

joiner strip

joiner strip

PROTEA QUEEN ©1994 CENTER PETALS CUTTING PATTERN 1/8" cutting allowance included

DIAGONAL FOLD

3

2

DIAGONAL FOLD

PROTEA QUEEN ©1994 PETALS CUTTING PATTERN 1/8" cutting allowance included

PROTEA QUEEN ©1994 LEAF CUTTING PATTERN 1/8" cutting allowance included

DIAGONAL FOLD

1

STRAIGHT FOLD

CENTER

7"

Photocopy pattern and trace each pattern piece – include jointer strips for exact placement. Pattern includes 1/8" appliqué turn under allowance.

Determine size of fabric square needed to fit each pattern piece when they have each been folded into eighths.

Cut and fold fabric colors. Pin pattern in place. Cut pattern and joiner strip as indicated. The joiner strip will keep the pattern together for exact placement on background fabric. Cut it off when pattern pieces are pinned in place, before basting.

Fold background fabric into eighths, crease folds. First, center leaf into folds of background fabric. Following the numbers, overlap colors with the lowest numbers on top of one another. Sometimes a leaf will be over a flower stem, sometimes it will be under it. Flowers will be over stamens.

⬚ underlap of fabric colors

▥ joiner strip to be cut off after design is pinned in place

PROTEA QUEEN DESIGN

The leaf (1) goes over the petals (2) goes over the center petals (3). You can also make this a two color design by combining the petals 2 and 3.

BEGINNER PATTERN

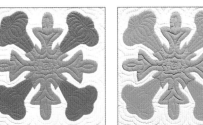

SUGGESTED QUILTING – EIGHTH OF THE DESIGN

PUA KENIKENI

The Hawaiian name means the "ten-cent flower" as the flowers were sold for ten cents each. The flowers at first bloom are white, aging to cream and a golden yellow. They are very fragrant and are a popular "special" lei flower.

Companion Piece:
Tuberose,
Page 57

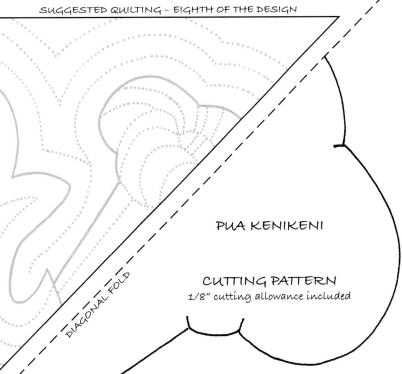

DIAGONAL FOLD

PUA KENIKENI

CUTTING PATTERN
1/8" cutting allowance included

PUA KENIKENI

©1994 Elizabeth Root | The Pillows to Patch Quilt Collection...the Hawaiian Way

CENTER

STRAIGHT FOLD

7"

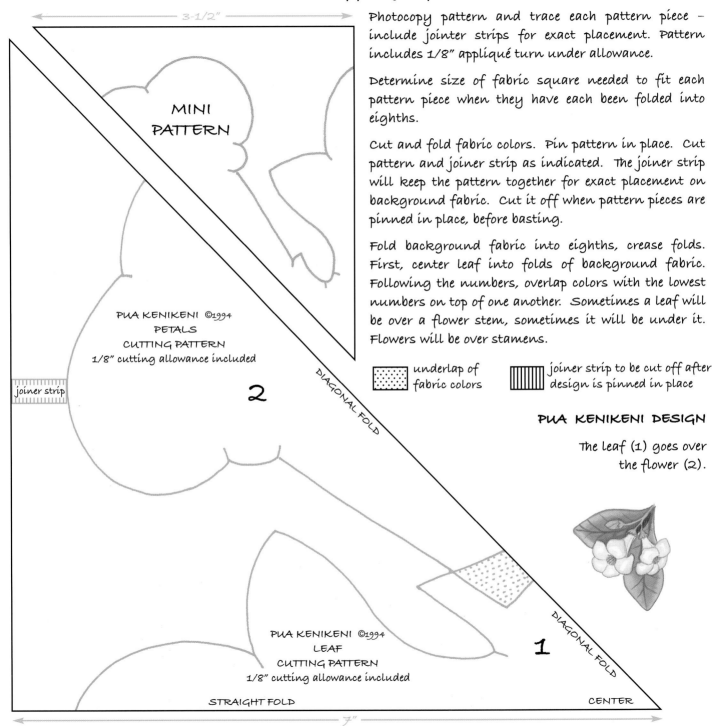

Photocopy pattern and trace each pattern piece – include jointer strips for exact placement. Pattern includes 1/8" appliqué turn under allowance.

Determine size of fabric square needed to fit each pattern piece when they have each been folded into eighths.

Cut and fold fabric colors. Pin pattern in place. Cut pattern and joiner strip as indicated. The joiner strip will keep the pattern together for exact placement on background fabric. Cut it off when pattern pieces are pinned in place, before basting.

Fold background fabric into eighths, crease folds. First, center leaf into folds of background fabric. Following the numbers, overlap colors with the lowest numbers on top of one another. Sometimes a leaf will be over a flower stem, sometimes it will be under it. Flowers will be over stamens.

underlap of fabric colors

joiner strip to be cut off after design is pinned in place

PUA KENIKENI DESIGN

The leaf (1) goes over the flower (2).

MINI PATTERN

PUA KENIKENI ©1994
PETALS
CUTTING PATTERN
1/8" cutting allowance included

joiner strip

2

DIAGONAL FOLD

PUA KENIKENI ©1994
LEAF
CUTTING PATTERN
1/8" cutting allowance included

1

DIAGONAL FOLD

STRAIGHT FOLD

CENTER

3-1/2"

7"

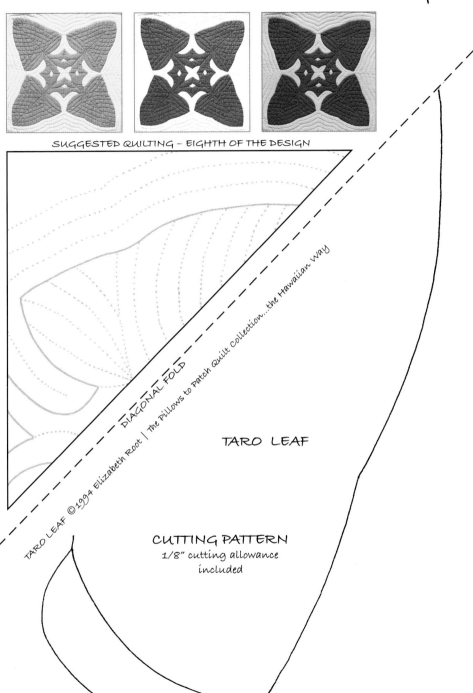

BEGINNER PATTERN

SUGGESTED QUILTING – EIGHTH OF THE DESIGN

TARO LEAF

One of the early Hawaiian food staples. Its tubers are made into poi, its leaves cooked like greens. The Hawaiians believed that it was brought by Wakea, Father Heaven and ancestor of all their chiefs. It is said that the menehunes (Hawaii's elves who work only at night) planted much of the taro in Hawaii because its cooked leaves along with shrimp and ferns were their favorite foods.

Companion Piece:
Autograph Leaf,
Page 10

DIAGONAL FOLD

TARO LEAF ©1994 Elizabeth Root | The Pillows to Patch Quilt Collection...the Hawaiian Way

TARO LEAF

CUTTING PATTERN
1/8" cutting allowance
included

CENTER   STRAIGHT FOLD

7"

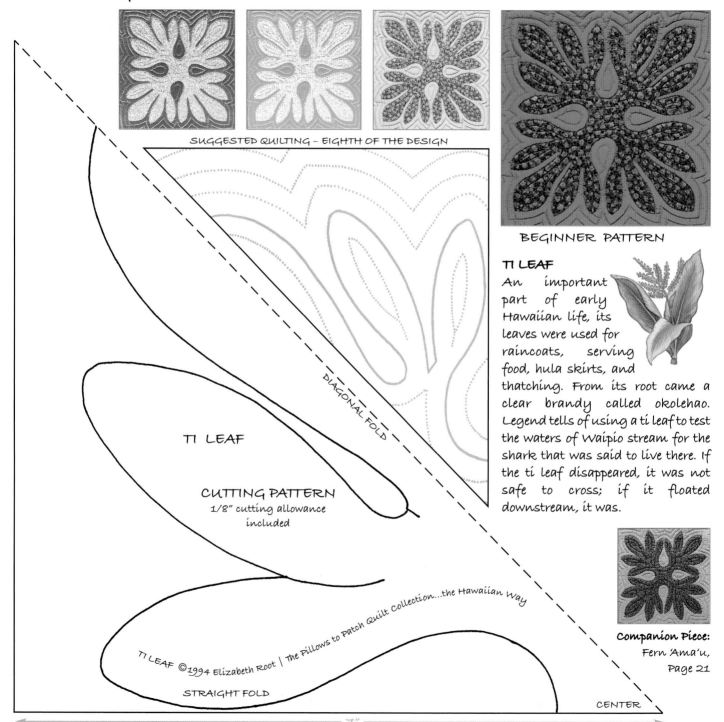

SUGGESTED QUILTING – EIGHTH OF THE DESIGN

BEGINNER PATTERN

DIAGONAL FOLD

TI LEAF

CUTTING PATTERN
1/8" cutting allowance
included

TI LEAF ©1994 Elizabeth Root | The Pillows to Patch Quilt Collection...the Hawaiian Way

STRAIGHT FOLD

CENTER

7"

TI LEAF

An important part of early Hawaiian life, its leaves were used for raincoats, serving food, hula skirts, and thatching. From its root came a clear brandy called okolehao. Legend tells of using a ti leaf to test the waters of Waipio stream for the shark that was said to live there. If the ti leaf disappeared, it was not safe to cross; if it floated downstream, it was.

Companion Piece:
Fern 'Ama'u,
Page 21

BEGINNER PATTERN

TUBEROSE

A wonderfully fragrant lei flower that grows on long flower-covered spikes originally from Mexico. It is grown commercially throughout Hawaii on small flower farms.

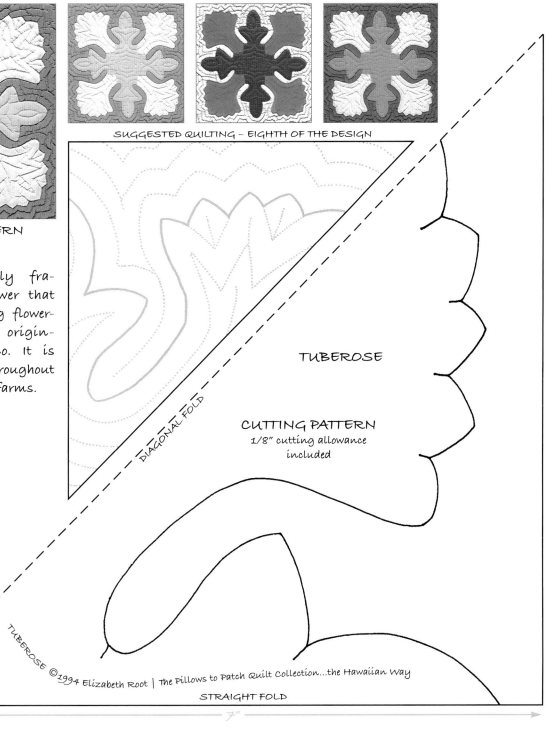

DIAGONAL FOLD

TUBEROSE

CUTTING PATTERN
1/8" cutting allowance
included

TUBEROSE ©1994 Elizabeth Root | The Pillows to Patch Quilt Collection...the Hawaiian Way

CENTER

STRAIGHT FOLD

7"

Companion Piece:
Pua Kenikeni,
Page 53

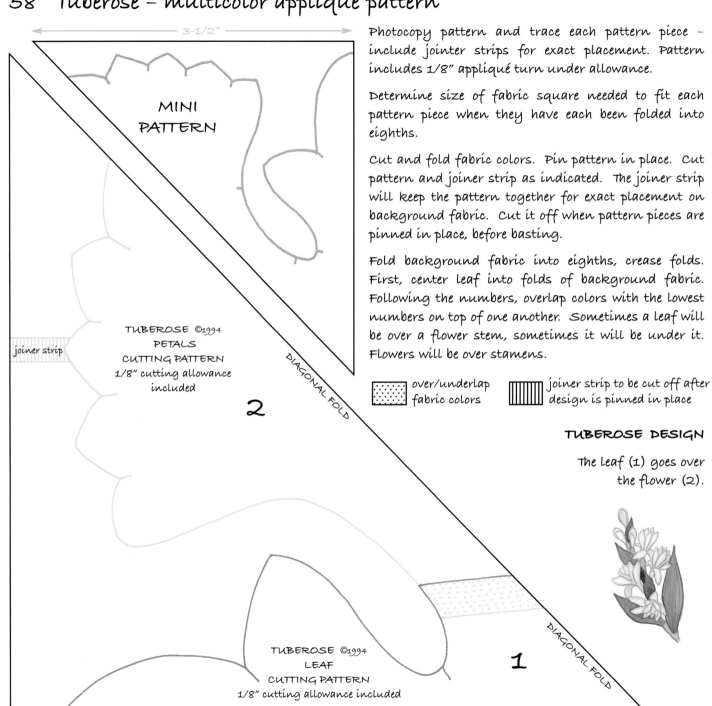

MINI PATTERN

3-1/2"

joiner strip

TUBEROSE ©1994
PETALS
CUTTING PATTERN
1/8" cutting allowance
included

2

DIAGONAL FOLD

TUBEROSE ©1994
LEAF
CUTTING PATTERN
1/8" cutting allowance included

1

DIAGONAL FOLD

STRAIGHT FOLD

CENTER

7"

Photocopy pattern and trace each pattern piece – include jointer strips for exact placement. Pattern includes 1/8" appliqué turn under allowance.

Determine size of fabric square needed to fit each pattern piece when they have each been folded into eighths.

Cut and fold fabric colors. Pin pattern in place. Cut pattern and joiner strip as indicated. The joiner strip will keep the pattern together for exact placement on background fabric. Cut it off when pattern pieces are pinned in place, before basting.

Fold background fabric into eighths, crease folds. First, center leaf into folds of background fabric. Following the numbers, overlap colors with the lowest numbers on top of one another. Sometimes a leaf will be over a flower stem, sometimes it will be under it. Flowers will be over stamens.

over/underlap fabric colors

joiner strip to be cut off after design is pinned in place

TUBEROSE DESIGN

The leaf (1) goes over the flower (2).

...

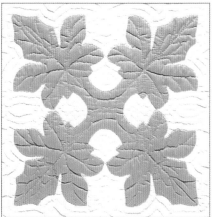

BEGINNER PATTERN

WOODROSE LEAF

The woodrose, actually woody petal-like enlarged sepals that look like an open rose, is used in dried arangements. The vine-like plant has these wonderfully shaped leaves.

Companion Piece:
Gourd Leaf,
Page 29

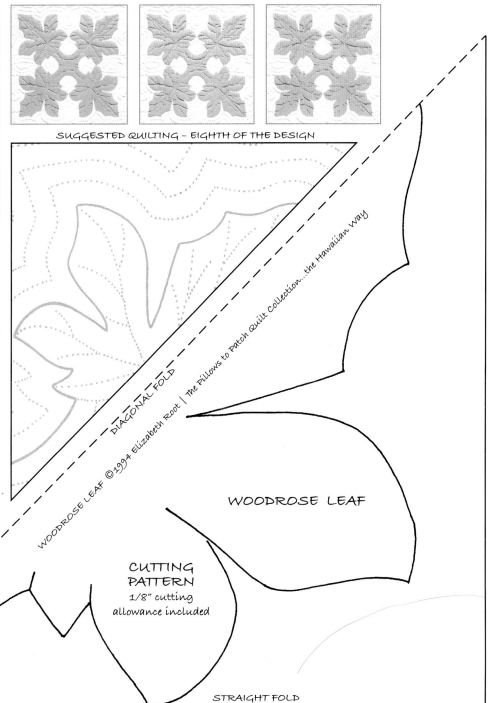

SUGGESTED QUILTING – EIGHTH OF THE DESIGN

DIAGONAL FOLD

WOODROSE LEAF ©1994 Elizabeth Root | The Pillows to Patch Quilt Collection...the Hawaiian Way

WOODROSE LEAF

CUTTING PATTERN
1/8" cutting allowance included

CENTER

STRAIGHT FOLD

Just Some Suggestions

 Yes, Hawaiian-style appliqué and quilting can be done by machine. But handiwork looks SO much better. As with all handmade quilts, it's the time, the thoughts and spirit of the quilter that shines as brightly as the design.

 Depending upon the project you want to create all the designs (including the mini's) can be enlarged. The primary designs in this book were all made 18 inches square. The beginner designs can be enlarged to make up to 27" blocks (150% enlargement) and the intermediate and advanced designs can be enlarged for 35" blocks (200% enlargement).

 Choosing your fabrics. Buy the best quality materials you can afford. You will be investing a lot of time and effort in the making of your Hawaiian-style quilt masterpiece. By the time you're finished, you'll want it to last a lifetime...maybe longer.

 Choosing your colors. Traditionally, two highly contrasting solid colors are used. There is no right or wrong color combination. Use your favorite colors or whatever blends best with your decor. Color can be bold and highly contrasting; subtle and pastel; two of the same color family, one light and one dark, or multiple colors. Fabrics can be solids, prints, textures, cotton, chintz, silk, whatever strikes your fancy. There is no right or wrong choice.

 Choosing your quilting style. Traditionally, echo style is used. But you can also use any quilting design that you like or that better suits the look of the finished piece. Many times a very lacy, delicate, busy, appliqué design looks better with a cross hatch (small squares) behind it to accentuate the design. Early quilts used a variety of quilting patterns.

 When quilting next to the appliquéd design, always quilt right against the turned-under fabric. This makes the design appear a little raised above the background fabric.

 Your mood will be reflected in your stitching. Calm and happy or angry and annoyed - your mood will show in your stitching. A little calm quilting each day and you will finish in no time. Above all, enjoy what you're doing. Quilt and chat and laugh with friends.

 Despite how anxious you are to see the finished piece, don't rush your work. From start to finish, time taken to ensure each step is properly done will save you time and disappointment later on.

Make your own Hawaiian Quilt Masterpiece

Quilter's Paradise

First,
go shopping...
...at your favorite quilt
or fabric shop

The List

1) Pattern - Get first so I can decide on fabric.

2) Fabric for appliqué design and contrasting for background & backing.

3) Thread - Good cotton same color as design for appliqué. Thread to quilt - either white or same color as background.

4) Needles #8 or #9 sharps or same size milliners (longer) for appliqué. #7 - #9 betweens for quilting.

5) Sharp scissors to cut out pattern; smaller pair for snipping/cutting while working.

6) Straight pins silk or dressmaker pins are good.

7) Thimble

8) Silver-colored pencil or chalk for marking quilt lines.

9) Quilting hoop - Make sure it's strong and smooth.

10) Get extra piece of muslin to back pillow batting. Zipper, cording (optional) to make pillow.

11) Get cat treats at market.

Next,
select your pattern
and fabric and get all
your supplies.

Cutting, pinning and basting

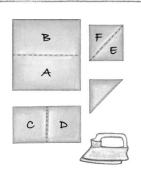

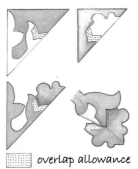

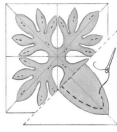

overlap allowance

enlarged

Prewash, iron, cut, fold appliqué/background fabric, right sides up, as shown.
1. Fold A up to B.
2. Fold C over to D.
3. Fold E up to F.
4. Iron in folds on both fabrics.

Place pattern on fabric, as shown. Pin through all layers OR trace around pattern with a pencil, then pin. Cut out design.

If making a multi-colored design: follow the pattern and cut each color separately. Add enough fabric to allow for overlapping elements, e.g. flower under or stem; basket over stem.

Open folded, cut appliqué/background fabrics, right sides up. Ease appliqué folds to match background folds and your design is automatically centered.

Pin design to background, without stretching fabric. Keep folds lined up as possible. Baste 1/4" inside edge of appliqué. Keep fabrics smooth, and wrinkle free. Remove pins.

JUST A SUGGESTION
With these first steps, it is very important to be as precise as possible as they are the foundation of your finished work. Cutting without letting the layers slip, smoothing the design gently from the center outward so it is flat against the background before pinning and basting, ensures problem-free appliqué and quilting later on.

Appliqué

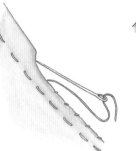 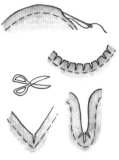 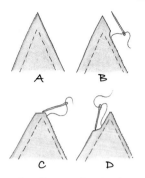  

Patterns allow for an average 1/8" turn-under. Use the 1/4" basting line as a guide and turn fabric under until it hits basting stitches. Use the tip of your needle to help turn under the fabric ahead as you appliqué.

Ease fabric under, without stretching it, for outside curves. Inside curves and valleys: snip as needed to help ease fabric under neatly. Always take extra stitches at the snips to prevent fraying.

A) Points, as in the tips of leaves. B) Appliqué up one side to 2 or 3 stitches from point. C) Turn point under, cut away excess fabric if needed, but always try to allow 1/8" turn under. D) Fold under remaining side and appliqué.

Cutouts and slits. Mark desired appliqué line around cutout or slit and appliqué using inside curve and valley methods. You may opt not to make cutouts and slits in a design.

Appliqué the entire design. Take out basting stitches. Look over your appliqué work and see if it needs to be cleaned. If so, wash in warm water with ivory flakes. Gently iron.

JUST A SUGGESTION

Appliqué using a single thread about 18" long to prevent tangling. Use the same color thread as the design color to help hide the stitches. Strive for no less than 8 appliqué stitches per inch. It's okay to snip fabric to help you turn it under more easily, but then, always take a few extra stitches to prevent fabric from fraying. Take an extra stitch at the tip of a point.

Quilting

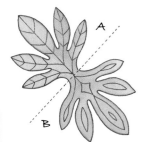

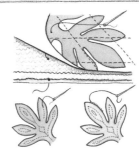

Follow the suggested quilting lines on the pattern selected or design your own quilting lines. Make the appliqué quilting: A) realistic, or B) echo style. Background quilting is traditionally echo style.

For a wall hanging, layer appliqué on batting, batting on back-ing fabric. For a pillow, use muslin as backing. Save backing fabric for pillow back. Cut batting at least 2" larger all around than fabric squares.

Pin layers together, smooth fabric from center as you pin toward the edge. Baste layers together in a grid pattern. Keep smoothing layers, pin as necessary. When finished, remove pins.

With the first stitch, catch the knot of a single thread in the batting. First quilt the appliquéd design. The first row of quilting on the background goes right against the appliquéd edge. Quilt around the appliqué.

Continue to quilt toward the edges. When quilted, remove basting stitches. Trim batting. You are ready to finish the quilt block as a pillow, wall hanging, or any way you wish.

JUST A SUGGESTION

Start with no fewer than eight stitches per inch; that's four on the front and four on the back. As you gain more control over your needle, set your goal at 16 to 20 stitches per inch. It is more important to make your stitches and spaces even than to make tiny stitches with large spaces. Quilt rows should be a consistent width – 1/2" to 3/4" wide or as small as 1/4" for miniatures.

PILLOWS

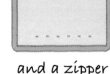

The simplest way of finishing a pillow is to put the right sides of the quilted square and the backing fabric together. Sew around three sides and four corners, leaving enough room to add your pillow form. Hand stitch the opening closed.

You can also add cording

and a zipper to the back

Other things to do with your Hawaiian-style quilt masterpieces...

Euro Pillow for your bed...Futons for the floor...Add multiple borders for larger wall hangings...Put multiple blocks of the same or different designs together for even larger wall hangings or a long wall hanging above a couch or bed...Put two blocks together with shoulder straps for a great quilter's tote to hold your work in progress.

Wall Hangings

Adding a sleeve

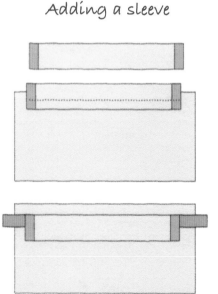

Cut a width of fabric the same size as your finished wall hanging. It is best to use the same color. Seam the edges with a one-inch allowance on both sides. With right sides together, hand sew the top of the strip to the top of the quilt. Then fold fabric down and sew the bottom to the back of the quilt. This will make a sleeve to hold a rod to hang your quilt.

Measure the width of the wall hanging. Determine how many hanging tabs are needed.

For three inches showing above your wall hanging, cut out 10" x 3" strips. Sew a 1/2-inch turn seam all around (A). Fold in half. (B), right sides out, hand sew them an equal distance apart, through both layers, to the back of your wall hanging. Thread the rod through them to hang.

Adding tabs

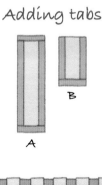

A

B

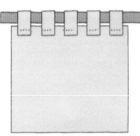

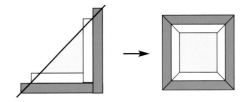

ADDING BORDERS - MITERING CORNERS

To add multiple borders, you will want to miter the corners for the best look. Determine the width of your border(s). Cut four strips the length of each side with a 4" allowance. Additional strips should be cut to that length plus an additional 4" each. With each border you add, remember that the length will be getting longer.

If making multiple borders sew them together first. With right sides facing, sew the borders to the sides of the front of the quilt square corner to corner.

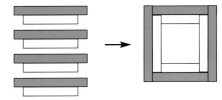

When all four sides have been sewn, fold the square in half diagonally. Line up the seams of the borders and stitch diagonally across, joining them. Refold the other way and sew remaining two corners. Cut off excess and press.

Be sure to make your backing fabric large enough to cover the back, including the borders. The outside edge of both the border and the backing fabric need to allow for a 1/2" seam allowance. Place right sides of fabric together and seam around three sides and four corners, leaving just enough open along the fourth side to turn inside out and sew closed by hand. Or, you can add an inch and a half to the width last border and turn the fabric to the back and sew all around on the back.

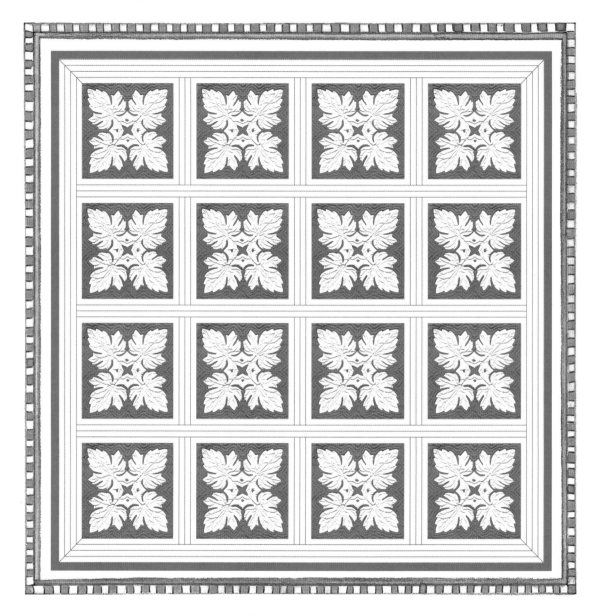

Blue & White Gourd Leaf Quilt
made using individual blocks joined together with decorative border added

Joining multiple quilt blocks using inner border strips

Always plan your inner border widths in proportion to the size of the blocks. It's always good to lay out the blocks with the inner border strips before joining them to make sure they blend together nicely. Stand back several feet to get the finished effect. If the borders jump out at you (and that's not the desired effect), then try other colors to find what works best.

Join A, B, C allowing a 1/2" seam line

To make rows like this

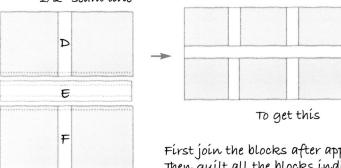

Join D, E, F allowing a 1/2" seam line

To get this

First join the blocks after appliquéing. Then quilt all the blocks individually to the edge of the borders, then quilt the border with its own pattern.

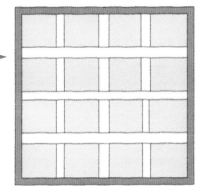

Add quilt binding and finish

Adding your own label

Made by: Elizabeth & Kym
For our friend: Tammy Yee -
for her home in Kaneohe, Hawaii
Finished: March 17, 2002
Design: Blue & white Gourd Leaf

Kym
Miller
2002

You've spent countless hours and great effort creating your Hawaiian quilt masterpiece - take credit for it. Add a pretty label showing the name of the design, your name, and the date finished. If it is a gift, you can add the name of the recipient and the occasion. At least embroider your name and date on the bottom back corner of the quilt and it will follow your masterpiece as it gathers history.

70 Leaf Mini Patterns

1/8" cutting allowance is included

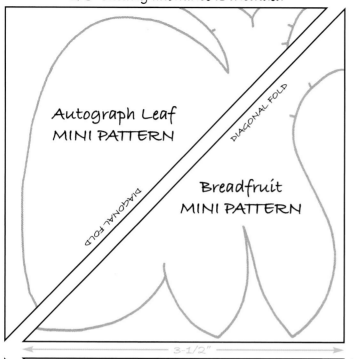

Autograph Leaf
MINI PATTERN

DIAGONAL FOLD

DIAGONAL FOLD

Breadfruit
MINI PATTERN

← 3-1/2" →

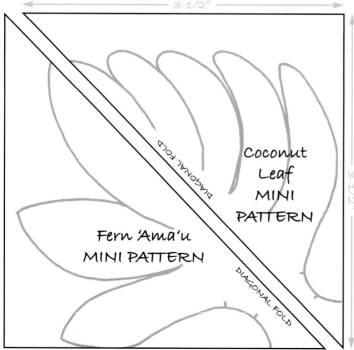

DIAGONAL FOLD

Coconut
Leaf
MINI
PATTERN

Fern 'Ama'u
MINI PATTERN

DIAGONAL FOLD

3-1/2"

1/8" cutting allowance is included

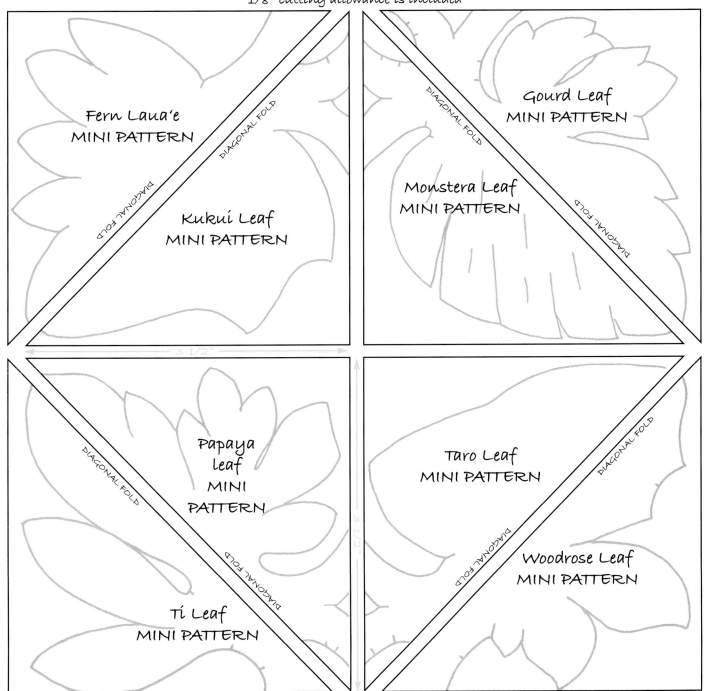

Fern Laua'e
MINI PATTERN

DIAGONAL FOLD

DIAGONAL FOLD

Kukui Leaf
MINI PATTERN

DIAGONAL FOLD

Gourd Leaf
MINI PATTERN

DIAGONAL FOLD

Monstera Leaf
MINI PATTERN

3 1/2"

DIAGONAL FOLD

DIAGONAL FOLD

Papaya
leaf
MINI
PATTERN

Ti Leaf
MINI PATTERN

3 1/2"

Taro Leaf
MINI PATTERN

DIAGONAL FOLD

DIAGONAL FOLD

Woodrose Leaf
MINI PATTERN

About the "WOW"

We, the "Windward Oahu Wahines," have had fun putting this book together for you. A little rest and we'll be on to the next...

Elizabeth Root is a designer, author and publisher of numerous Hawaiian design quilt and counted cross stitch books. She lives, servant to several rescued cats, on the windward side of Oahu.

Also look for "Menehune Quilts... the Hawaiian Way" – 20 new, original Hawaiian quilt designs for 24" miniatures

Tammy Yee is an author and illustrator of several children's books with Hawaiian themes. She lives with her physician husband, Ric, and two young sons, Cosmo and Bobby, on the windward side of Oahu.

We'd be delighted if you could visit us via the internet at www.quiltshawaii.com and www.TammyYee.com